THE FARMBOY

IN 1950'S PALERMO, ONTARIO

THE FARMBOY

IN 1950'S PALERMO, ONTARIO

"REMEMBERING"

MY LIFE ON THE FARM

Wayne E Shillum – Author

DEDICATED

This book is dedicated to my parents

And my brothers Robert L. Shillum and Brian D. Shillum

Robert Henry Shillum   Rose Violet Shillum   Me and my Brothers

My Dad   My Mom   The Shillum Boys

Brian is in front, Bob is in the Middle, I am at the back

In 1950, my parents decided that they wanted to provide more for their three sons than growing up in the city.

They had a lot of just plain guts to take on the task of managing a 100-acre dairy farm in Palermo, Ontario with no prior experience.

This was done while my dad held on to a full-time sales job in Toronto, Ontario. This would provide the entire family with an adventure in the small village of rural Palermo Ontario that has now, all but disappeared.

Table of Contents

WHY WAS THIS WRITTEN

IT WAS WRITTEN FOR MY OWN CHILDREN

Ryan W Shillum

And

Tracey L Shillum

I retired in 2011, and after writing a few books on Sales and Marketing, I was looking for a change.

My daughter said "Dad you are always talking about your childhood on the farm. Why don't you write about it?"

So, I did.

WHAT IT IS ABOUT

This book is about my early years on a farm in Palermo, Ontario. It describes what it was like farming in the 50's, and what the small village of Palermo was like during the 1950's as well.

In 1950, at age of six, I moved with my parents along with my brothers Brian age three, and Bob age twelve. We left the city life in Toronto to live on a 100-acre dairy farm in Palermo, Ontario.

Here we all would experience a life style that has now pretty much vanished along with the village. In the beginning we would farm using only horse drawn machinery which we describe in detail.

The lifestyle still exists within the Amish and Mennonite communities. Today in 2018, trips to Elmira, Ontario area; bring back many memories of my childhood.

From 1950 to 1955, I would attend Grades one to six at Palermo Public #2. It was a one room school with one teacher for the early years and would eventually reach two teachers for the eight grades.

In 1956, we would leave the one room school to attend a new 4 room school "Palermo Public # 3 with four teachers.

This book ends when I graduated from grade eight. Life would change dramatically when starting High School in Oakville at Thomas A. Blakelock.

Our farming would go through many changes during those early years and by the sixties, I would see our farm and rural community way of life begin to fade into History.

This book covers those changes from 1950 to 1958

List of Contributors

Trafalgar Historical Society Palermo

Trafalgar Township Historical Society

Trafalgar Township 1955

www.tths.ca/palermo.htlm

www.tths.ca

www.oakville.ca

www.oakvillehistory.org

Trafalgar Township Historical Society – Old Palermo one room

Oakville Heritage Society

Google Search – Palermo Historical Society

Palermo, Ontario.ca 1900

Images.

Pinterest, eBay, NCSU Libraries, Jeffersoncountryiowa.com, you tube,

Smallfarmersjournal.ca, Wikipedia, kristiekandoll.com, Buyers Guide,

wisconsinhistory.com, southwestpost.ca, borculo.weebly.com,

wisconsonhistory.org, Big Chill, farmcollector.com, bidspotter,

ruralheritage.com, Alberta Estonian Heritage, bidspotter, edenhillswordpress.com, pinsdaddy.com,

Google search, Google Images,

People

My brother Brian Shillum, My niece Tammy A, My cousin John Shillum,

Disclaimer

This book was written for my two children to provide them with information about my life on the farm. In the process of gathering information, I have relied on the sources listed on the previous contributor's page.

I have not knowingly used any copyrighted materials and have used material available as part of the public domain. I have listed all sources where the material and pictures were obtained.

The book is not meant to represent a complete historical document, and lists the names that I knew as residents, during my days on the farm from 1950 to 1958.

During my research I discovered many fascinating articles on the early beginnings of Palermo. I have included some of these when describing the village.

THE VERY EARLY YEARS

Before the Farm

We had moved to Toronto from London Ontario where I was born in 1944, at St Joseph's hospital. I do not remember the move to Toronto as I was somewhere between 2 and 3 at the time.

My dad had accepted a sales job in Toronto for a paint company called Berry Brothers. While his office was in Toronto, his territory was Ontario.

My memories of the first years in Toronto are somewhat of a blur. This is partly because of my young age. During the last 2 years in Toronto, some things do stand out in my mind.

We had lived at the north end of Toronto just north of the Eglington and Avenue Road intersection (east of Avenue rd.). I remember the street and house mostly from re-visiting.

We took trips to the city with my Mom about every 2 weeks to do her grocery shopping for many years after the move to the farm.

We had lived on a street called Roselawn Ave. in a duplex numbered 313. We were at the top end of the street on the south side. The house was on a large hill with a park at the bottom.

Just north of us on Roselawn, was some sort of military base (I think air force).

In Our Toronto Backyard

Brian and me   Bob, Brian, a friend and me

Toronto Memories

I remember attending baseball games with my parents in the park at the bottom of our street. Here my friends and I would also fly kites and model airplanes and shoot our arrows across the park when no one was around.

I remember attending a Major League baseball game and seeing Jackie Robinson play. Upon returning home I threw a ball through the kitchen window, which ended my baseball career for a while.

I remember being fascinated with matches and starting a fire that burned a huge hole in my neighbour's garage. The punishment was a visit to the local fire hall. Once there, I had to apologize to Captain Sheldon for my deeds.

His name would be burned into my memory forever.

I had a tour of the fire hall and had to make apologies to all the firemen who had helped to put out the fire. I never played with matches again.

I remember venturing onto a garage roof where my friend Leonard; dressed in his superman costume from Halloween, would make an unsuccessful attempt to fly. Upon his landing, he broke his leg.

I was dressed as Robin Hood and knew I could not fly.

Throwing stones at passing cars would be a short-term pastime for Leonard and me. It ended when a lady was hit in the head with a stone through her open window.

This time the authorities (police) visited us. I got a warning from the policeman.

My dad arranged a visit to the jail and a lock-up for about 10 minutes (my dad's idea of constructive punishment). At age six it made a huge impact on me.

I did not ever want to end up there. This time I got the strap from my dad. This was a punishment not used by him, on most disciplinary actions.

He was more into a constructive form of discipline through examples. I was cured and never threw stones at cars or anyone again.

My first experiences in school was kindergarten in a huge city school. I remember how large the classroom was. There were more classmates than I could imagine.

I remember having to pee so bad that I used someone's rubber boot. I did not own up when the teacher asked who was to blame. She was so angry, it made sense to keep quiet.

The Search for a Country Home

After my dad had successfully established himself in his new job, he and my mom decided that growing up in the country would a perfect life for their three boys.

Perhaps my activities had some influence on their motives. I prefer to think that it was not the main reason for the move.

I remember the search for the right farm and the different inspections of houses and barns. For some reason, I still remember two small twin goats at one farm. They were called "This" and "That"

The explanation of how the owners could tell them apart was: *"This" had that feature and "That" had this feature.*

It was a very funny clarification and confusing. This was my choice (probably because of the goats), but it did not happen.

MOVING DAY MEMORIES 1950

It was early summer in 1950 and I had turned 6 in March. My parents had purchased a 100 Acre dairy farm that was one concession north of Palermo on the Back Concession, just west of Hwy 25 (Bronte Rd).

My brother Brian and I differ on what we think they had paid. Brian says $15,000 and I thought $30,000. Either amount seems ridiculously low by today's real estate values.

The purchase price included the 100 acres, house, barn and implement buildings, about 12 milking cows some chickens, two work horses (Frank and Laudie), a riding horse (Trigger), two dogs (Laddie and Lassie), and all the equipment needed to farm (described later).

It also included all the items described in our initial exploration of the house upon our arrival and inspection.

The Arrival

Moving day had finally arrived, and with it the beginning of our country adventure. I still remember in vivid detail the events of our arrival as we turned west off highway #25 (then not paved) onto another dirt side road.

This side-road was called "The Back Concession". It would later become and still is Burnhamthorpe Road.

As we started down the first large hill my dad anxiously pointed to a house and barn on the north side (right side) at the top of the second hill and said: *"There is our new home"*.

As we turned into the driveway, we passed through a large open wire gate with large concrete block posts on either side.

The gate had a tubular frame of about one and one-half inches in diameter. It was 6 inches off the ground about 48 inches high by about 14 feet wide.

The Entrance

The House

On the right side of the driveway (east side) was a large two story white frame house with green shutters and a green shingled roof.

I remember noticing three strange long pointed metal rods on the roof that pointed upwards to the sky. (lightning rods)

The entire house and lawn area was enclosed with a wire fence complete with white fence posts. There was a small wire pedestrian gate allowing access from the driveway to the house.

A partial view of the gate and pathway in

The Entrance to the house and the horse Pepper

To the left in the picture above is a partial view of the wire gate and the wood planks on the dirt pathway to the house.

More Cousins

Note: Fence on west Lawn
And the gateway to the House

RAMPS TO 2ND FLOOR

NORTH

LANEWAY

BARN

EQUIPMENT STAGING

BARN YARD

GARAGE

IMPLEMENT BARN

SHEDS

HOUSE

WELLS

BACK CONCESSION 1950   DRIVEWAY IN   BURNHAMTHORPE ROAD 1967

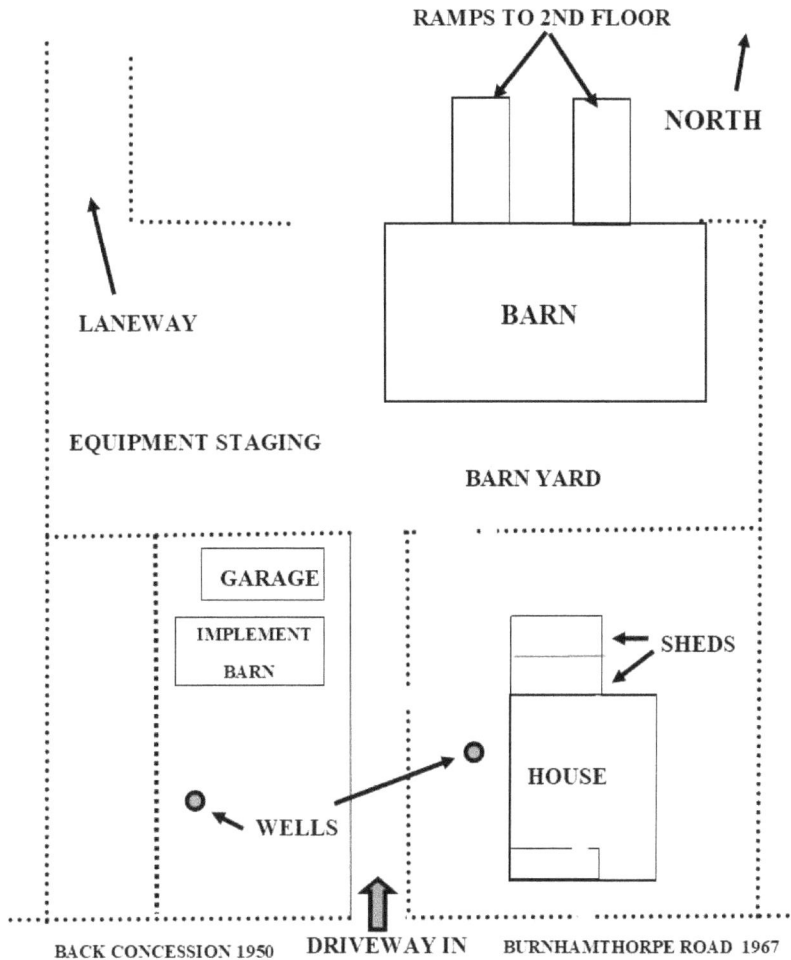

The Exploration Begins

As we got out of the car, we were greeted by the previous owner Fred E. and he immediately pointed out some danger areas.

There were two wells. One was beside the house and the other was on the other side of the driveway. They were loosely covered with old wooden boards and had hand operated pumps on the top of each of them. A third danger point would be an inground cistern inside the front shed.

The House and Grounds in 1950

The area allotted for the house, lawns and gardens was on the east side of the driveway. It was about 150 feet wide by 200 feet deep running from the road north to the barnyard.

All four sides of the house lot were enclosed by a wire fence attached to the faded white 6-inch diameter cedar fence posts.

The front (south) fence next to the road, was lined with lilac and pine trees. A single large maple tree was centrally located.

In the middle of this front fence, between the lilac trees and maple was a gate leading out to the road. A two-inch thick x 12-inch wide plank acted as a bridge over the ditch to the road.

On the south west corner of the house lot (east of driveway), stood an elm tree, that would reach considerable size in the years to come.

Moving north along the west fence, there was a small maple tree, followed by several small pine trees. Next came a larger maple tree. Just before the gate to the house were several smaller pine trees.

The gate was the access to the house by way of a dirt path. The wire fence continued to the back of the house lot with a few smaller pine trees lining it.

Running east across the north fence, at the back of the lot, was a second gate. It was about 12 to 14 feet wide for equipment access to the house lot. Just past the large gate was another small gate for people access to the barnyard.

The lawns on the south, west and north sides of the house resembled a freshly cut hay field. This was mainly because they had just been cut prior to our arrival, by the horse drawn mower used to cut hay.

On all four sides of the house, were large overgrown flower gardens. The entire east lawn was overgrown with shrubs, trees and high grass. The north lawn behind the house, had a small vegetable garden.

It was time to start exploring our new home. Opening the access gate from the driveway, we travelled up a dirt path to the house.

A large worn wood platform in front of the door provided an area to remove boots if required. We would first enter what was called the front shed.

LAYOUT FIRST FLOOR OF HOUSE

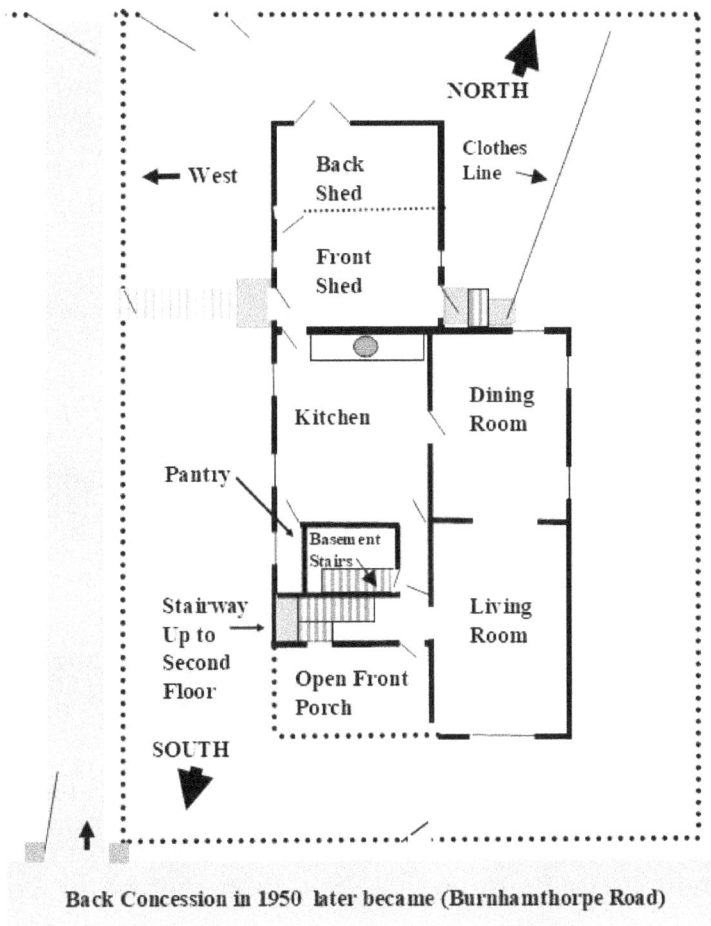

Back Concession in 1950 later became (Burnhamthorpe Road)

Exploring the House

The Front Shed

Access to the front shed would be through two doors. The first was a screen door and the second was a green wooden door.

The front shed was the change area for the rubber boots and coveralls that were used for barn duty. We were immediately greeted with the unmistakable odour of cow manure.

Our Farm Life Had Officially Started

This front shed was about 12 to 15 feet wide (north to south) by 25 feet long (east to west). It had a linoleum covered wood floor.

Just inside the front shed door and immediately to the right, was the main entrance door to the house. About 8 feet to our left side, was the door to the back shed.

Danger Area #3

The third danger area was in the front shed. It was the floor access door for the cistern. This in-ground concrete cistern contained rain water collected by the eves trough on all four sides of the house.

The water was used for domestic household cleaning. The covering was in very bad condition and would not support anyone standing on it. A chair had been put in front of it and sectioned off using twine.

The previous owner was a widower with no children. This explained why the two wells and the floor access door had not been child proofed. They would be immediately placed on the things-to-do list.

Along the right side of the front shed wall (south side) was where all the work clothing was hung.

The left side (north side) of the shed, was a storage area for all sorts of things; including, garden tools and scythes for cutting the weeds and a host of other maintenance items.

Walking across the shed to the opposite side (the east side) was another door. It mirrored the door we had just entered.

To the left of the door on the east door was a small window. About half way down the east wall, there was a small oil-fired stove for heating the shed during the cold months.

The door on the east side of the shed opened to the east lawn. Just outside that door, another wood platform acted as a place to stand and put on or remove boots.

Outside and further eastward along the house exterior wall, was a raised platform (2 to 3 steps high) to access the clothes line.

Outside, on the east side of the front shed wall, was a large tank containing stove oil for the stove.

The Back Shed

On the north/west corner of the front shed was a door to the back shed. This shed acted as an intermediate garbage and dumping area as well as a storage area for the wood used in the kitchen stove.

It had a dirt floor that would later become a geological dig site for me. Here I would find old pots, old tools, and even some arrow heads.

The Kitchen

The kitchen access door was immediately to the right upon entering the front shed on the west side. The kitchen door had a frosted glass section in the upper part with white lace curtains.

The kitchen itself was a typical huge country kitchen about 25 feet by 25 feet in size with a 10-foot ceiling.

A single socket light fixture provided the only lighting in the room except for the two very large windows to the right on the west wall. They also allowed viewing of the west side yard.

The Walk in Pantry

Straight ahead was a door to the walk-in pantry. The pantry was about 15 feet deep x 6 feet wide. It had a 24-inch-deep floor-to-ceiling cupboard at the south end of it.

The pantry had a single hanging light with a pull chain switch. On the right west wall of the pantry was another large window. The pantry had hooks for clothing on the left and some shelving on the right.

The Panoramic view

As one started viewing the kitchen from the entrance doorway, in a counter-clockwise manner along the west wall; the first thing that met the eye was an ice cooled refrigerator. It was between the two windows.

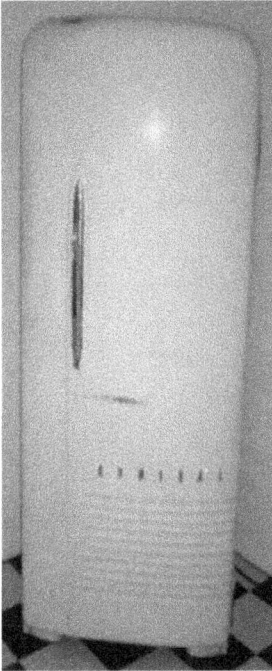

OUR ICE-COOLED FRIDGE

The fridge was kept cool with blocks of ice that we would get delivered each week.

Ice was available at the General store if we needed.

It would be a very big change from our electric one in Toronto

Next to the fridge was our old wooden crank telephone

One could contact anyone on our party line of 8 by simply turning the crank to achieve their designated signal.

The Fridge and Telephone came with the house

To reach people outside of the party line group, you had to contact the operator in the general store in Palermo. This was achieved by continuously turning the crank and waiting for the operator to answer.

If the operator was on lunch or a break, you just had to wait until they were back, to place your call. If it was after 12 Midnight; it usually meant waiting until 5 or 6AM the next day to place your call.

As I would discover at a later age, anyone on the party line could listen in on your conversations.

There was one person that would abruptly interrupt a conversation and tell you to get off the line. It was usually our neighbour on our east side (Mrs. "H") wanting to talk to her daughter Mrs. B (our neighbour across the road).

Mail Service – was at the Post Office in the Palermo General Store

The South Kitchen Wall

Continuing our viewing, from the south/west corner, were two galvanized tubs and next to them was the wringer washer.

Further to the left was the coal/wood stove that was used for heating the kitchen in the cooler weather but was also used for cooking until we got an electric stove.

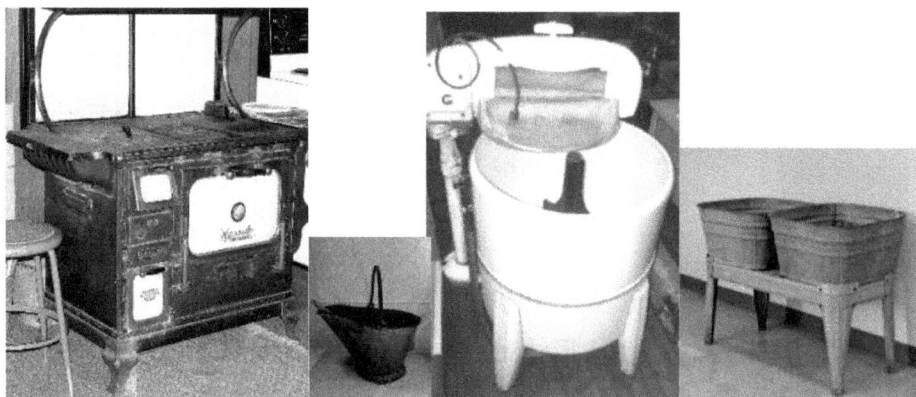

Wood Stove   Coal Scuttle   Washing Machine   Tubs
These also came with the House

It would soon become one of my many new chores to go down to the large pile of coal in the basement and fill the coal Scuttle. This trip was one I hated because the old dingy basement scared the "H" out of me.

The kitchen stove was a dual wood/coal stove and the trip to the back shed for wood was far less scary than travelling down into the old musty basement, unless it was after dark.

The Front Hallway

Just past the stove was a short hallway about 10 feet long that travelled south. The hallway contained 3 doors. One door was the entrance to the hallway.

On the right side of this hallway shown here, was the spooky door that opened down to the basement.

That door scared me, and I always passed quickly by it, in case something down there might grab me.

Straight ahead was a third door to the front hallway. A little further across the hallway was another glass-topped door with curtains. It opened out onto the open front porch area.

In the hallway when facing south, was another door opening into the living room on the left. There was a stairway to the right (west) that provided access to upstairs.

Back to the Kitchen

Continuing the scan of the kitchen from the stove and making a 90-degree left turn, we would travel north back along the east wall of the kitchen.

In the middle of the east kitchen wall was another door accessing the dining room. The 360-degree viewing would be completed by making another 90-degree turn to the left.

The North wall of the kitchen would reveal a wood counter running the full width of the room, except for the entrance doorway.

It had cupboards below the counter with curtains to hide their contents. Above the counter and stretching to the ceiling were open faced cupboards on each side of the sink area, for dishes and food.

In the middle of the painted wood counter was a sink with a sheet metal drain board to the left of it, for placing washed dishes.

On the right side of the sink was a hand pump that provided water for household use. Beside it was a jug containing water for priming.

In the wall behind the sink, was a large ceiling to floor drain pipe from the bathroom above.

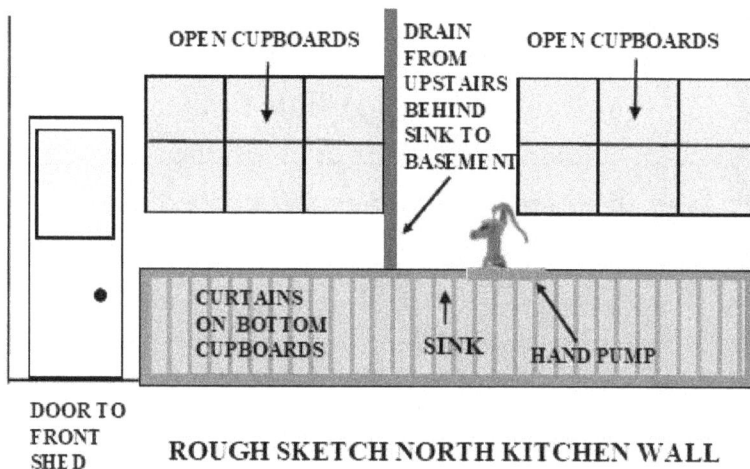

ROUGH SKETCH NORTH KITCHEN WALL

The Décor of the Kitchen

Wainscoting of 2-inch-wide wood tongue and groove, covered the lower part of the wall on the west, south and east sides of the kitchen.

It was about four feet high and painted a creamy white. Above it the walls were wallpapered with an obscenely large yellow flowered pattern.

The floor was covered with 3 lengths of linoleum. The first stretched into the pantry on the right. The second was in the middle. The third stretched down the hallway on the left side, to the front hallway.

The floor was very worn with many hastily made repairs that were not a very good fit or match.

In the middle of the room was a large double pedestal wooden kitchen table. When all the inserts were added the table was about 14 ft. long.

Dining Room

One entered the dining room through the doorway in the middle of the east kitchen wall.

The dining room was on the north-east side of the house. It had two large windows on the east wall and one at the back facing north providing a view of the barn.

The dining room and living room were separated with double glass doors.

The Living Room

The living room was on the south-east side. It had a large picture window on the south wall that looked out onto our front lawn and the road.

Heating of House

The house was heated by a large coal fired furnace in the basement. It was a true convectional furnace that supplied heat through a large floor grate in the centre of the living room floor.

THE FURNACE

The Coal-Fired Furnace

HOW IT WORKED

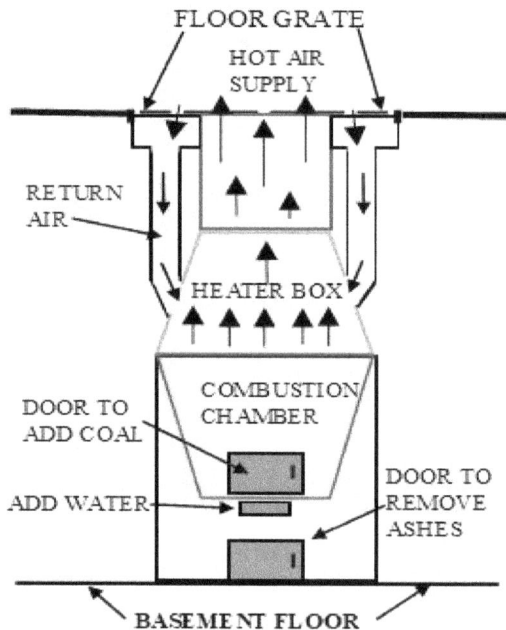

FLOOR GRATE

HOT AIR
SUPPLY

RETURN
AIR

HEATER BOX

COMBUSTION
CHAMBER

DOOR TO
ADD COAL

ADD WATER

DOOR TO
REMOVE
ASHES

BASEMENT FLOOR

The Components

The upper door on the front of the furnace was where we would shovel the coal to be burned. Below it was a small box in the furnace wall for adding water. (the humidifier)

Just below the humidifier were four or five short square metal rods protruding about 2 inches out from the furnace.

They could be turned using a small tool to sift the ashes to the bottom of the furnace.

The door at floor level was where the ashes were removed after the coal was burned. The jobs of adding water and coal and the removing of ashes, would become future chores for my brother Brian and me.

The Coal Pile

A truck would deliver the coal and send it down a chute through a basement window. The furnace and coal pile were in the east half of the basement.

The west half of the basement contained the stairway up, shelves for preserves and was the storage area for storm windows in the summer and screens in the winter.

The Living Room Floor Grate

The round centre section in the middle of the grate, was about 36 inches in diameter and was connected to the furnace plenum by ducting and acted as the supply of heated air.

The outer part was the cool air return which returned the air to the heating chamber to be re-heated. The grate was about five feet long by four feet wide.

The vacuum from the hot air rising in the supply duct and one-way dampers in the cool air return ducting, enabled the circulation pattern.

Top view of the 5' x 4' floor grate

The Convectional Heating System for the House

There were grate openings in the main floor ceiling to all the rooms upstairs to supply heat in the winter. The cool air would pretty much return down the stairs to the return section in the living room.

Winter Clothes Drying

The three-part clothes horse as we called it, would become a continuous drying station in the winter.

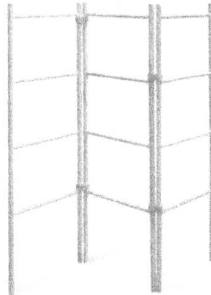

It would be placed on top of the round section for drying. We would hang our socks and mitts on it after returning from our winter recreational activities.

To the Second Floor

The hallway to the stairs was at the south end and could be accessed from the kitchen hallway or the living room.

The stairs were U-shaped with 3 to 4 steps running west to the first landing and turning right and running north another 3 – 4 steps that took you to the second landing.

Another turn to the right running east was the last part of about 10 to 12 steps that went to the second floor.

The Second Floor

At the top of the stairs, on the right or southside, there was a small landing about four feet wide running west along the edge of the stairwell.

A barrier of small one-inch diameter spindles about 40 – 48 inches in height, capped with a wood rail would run along the stairwell.

Four bedrooms would provide rooms for my parents myself and my two brothers.

Three bedrooms ran along the east side. The Southernmost would become my parents. My younger brother Brian would take possession of the middle one.

Mine would become the northern most one on the east side overlooking the barn. Bob my older brother would take the bedroom on the west side of the house.

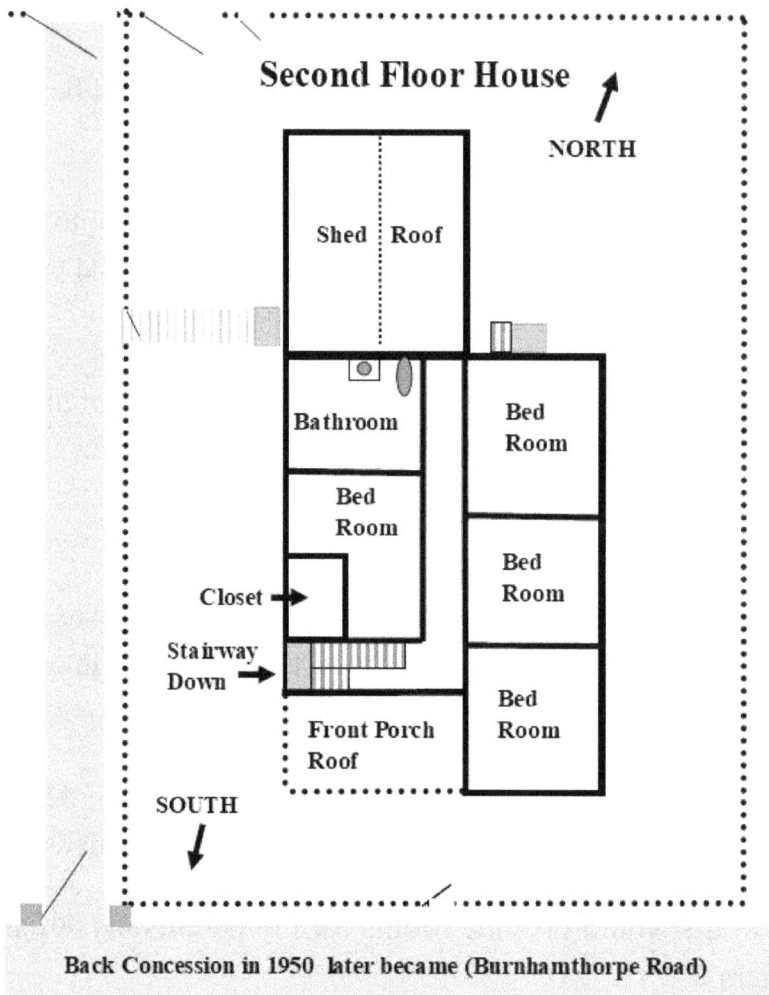

Second Floor House

NORTH

Shed : Roof

Bathroom

Bed Room

Bed Room

Bed Room

Closet →

Stairway Down →

Bed Room

Front Porch Roof

SOUTH

Back Concession in 1950 later became (Burnhamthorpe Road)

At the north end of the hallway to the left was the bathroom. The bath room would consist of a small sink and counter directly above the one in the kitchen.

On the counter would be another hand pump and container of water for priming the pump. The toilet was to the left (west) of the sink. Also, on the north wall to the far-left corner, was a small window.

There was no bath tub. Instead, we would take our baths in the kitchen in a large galvanized tub normally used by the cows for drinking. This would continue until my dad installed a bathtub.

In the middle of the south side of the bathroom; in the floor, there was a grate for suppling warm air from the kitchen stove. It was the main heat source for the bathroom.

Moving south along the hallway from the bathroom was another very large bedroom with a storage closet on the right (west side). This bedroom would be my older brother Bob's room.

During the day this room became a playroom. It is where I would encounter and play with two old ladies in hooped skirts who I believe were ghosts.

No one else would encounter them, but I was told years later that there had been two elderly sisters who had owned the property in the 1920's.

The entire upper floor was 6-inch pine flooring and was painted grey. Every room in the house was wallpapered (about 6 layers).

Moving In

The initial exploration was over as the moving Van had now arrived. Helping my mom with the unpacking would take up the remainder of our first day and part of the second.

The implement barn, garage, main barn and 100 acres would have to wait.

While we attended the unpacking, my dad would partake in his first lesson in the milking of our dairy herd of 12 Holsteins. Part of the purchase arrangement was for Fred (the previous owner) to help my dad through the initial learning stages of farming 101.

We had just stepped back in time to an early pioneer lifestyle. My dad had taken on an enormous task of rejuvenating a rundown dairy farm while still holding down a sales job in the city.

My mom had left behind many comforts to start a new life. She would be stepping back in time and living life with pioneer type amenities.

The house and grounds would need a lot of work to improve living conditions and upgrade to the 50's lifestyle.

For a six-year old it was like stepping into another world. There were so many sights and sounds. There were chickens walking about the barnyard and house lawns. The cows and three horses would be free to roam the enclosed barnyard.

So many buildings to explore
But, all this would have to wait

The Implement Barns

With the unpacking done, it was now time to start exploring the rest of the property. On the left side of the driveway (west side) and opposite the house, there was a large Implement barn and a small garage.

The Implement barn was about 20 feet wide by about 40 feet deep and 20 feet high. There were two large access doors facing the driveway.

It ran west from the driveway and was in a bad state of repair with questionable stability. It would be considered a danger area and off-limits for us.

Inside the Implement barn, were farm implements that we would later use. The support structure of both support columns and beams were hand hewn and were 14-inch x 14-inches square. The cross supports were also hand hewn and were about 4 inches by 4 inches.

The outside of the implement barn was covered with unpainted barn boards about 12 inches wide. The roof was peaked and covered with unpainted rusting corrugated steel.

The Garage

Beside the implement barn on the north side, stood a smaller garage with smaller corner posts and beams. It too was covered with barn boards. It also had a peaked corrugated steel roof.

We would discover later that inside the garage was an old model T Ford car, in running condition.

The Main Barn

Continuing north along the driveway one passed through the opening of the second wire gate also about 14 feet wide. Just ahead on the right side would be the main barn.

The Gateway to the Barn Area

EXTERIOR VIEW OF THE BARN 1950

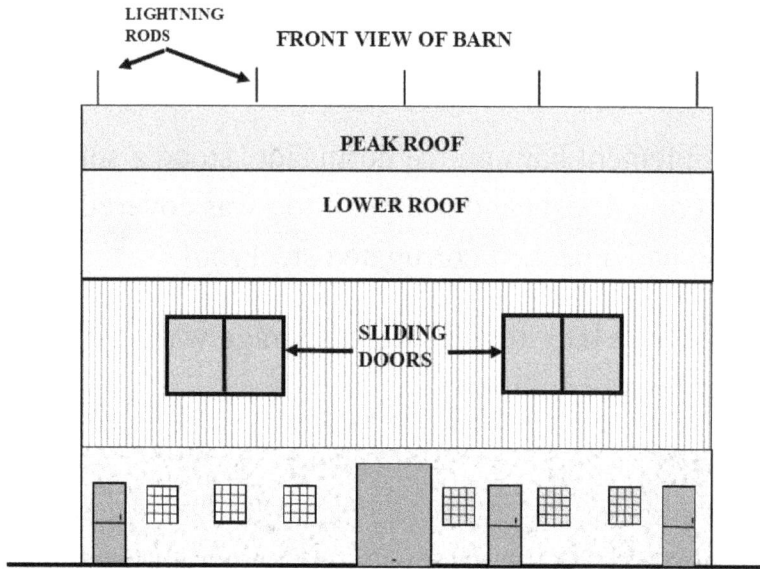

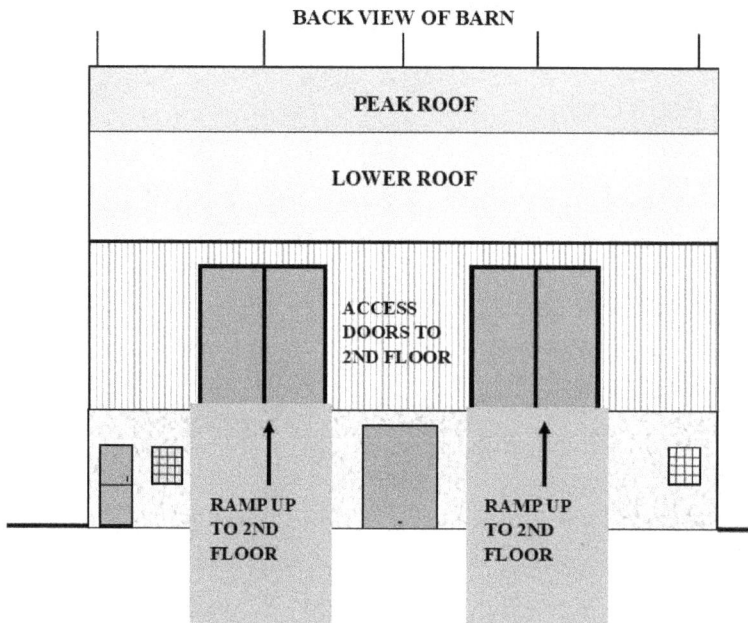

LIGHTNING
RODS

FRONT VIEW OF BARN

PEAK ROOF

LOWER ROOF

SLIDING
DOORS

BACK VIEW OF BARN

PEAK ROOF

LOWER ROOF

ACCESS
DOORS TO
2ND FLOOR

RAMP UP
TO 2ND
FLOOR

RAMP UP
TO 2ND
FLOOR

The barn was approximately 160 feet long by 65 feet wide by 60 feet high to the very peak.

The faded red barn needed a new paint job badly. The barn had a corrugated steel roof with many steel lightning rods along the top.

The barn was huge (the largest on our concession) and it dwarfed the rest of the buildings immediately around it.

Standing behind the house and facing the front or south side of the barn one viewed the 160-foot length.

View of Barn from East Lawn

View of House and Barn
looking East from West Front Field

Barn from West Side

Back of Barn

The Danger Areas of the Barn

Fred E and my dad would now show us the danger places in and around the barn.

Like the cistern in the house there was also one inside the barn. It was a large concrete pit in the floor with a 24-inch x 24-inch opening covered with 2-inch thick x 6-inch-wide boards that fit snugly in the recessed area.

On top of the boards, there was a small electrical pump for supplying the only water to the barn from the cistern.

Behind the barn under the east ramp, was a hand dug well with stone walls. It was covered loosely with old planks and would provide a dangerous outcome for anyone who walked on them. On top was a large hand pump. I do not think this well was ever used by us.

Under the west ramp was the milk house that had a cooler in the floor for cooling and storing milk cans until they were picked up.

After our danger 101 lessons, we were somewhat free to explore to explore the rest of the barn.

Front view

There were six windows along the ground level front of the barn. Each window had eight sections (panes). There were three windows on the east side of the large roll up door and three on the west side of the roll up door.

Man/Animal Doors

Facing the front of the barn, (south side), there was a large roll-up door in the middle.

There were three small barn doors with upper and lower sections, two on the east side and one on the west side. These doors allowed access to the lower barn area for people and animals without opening the large roll up door.

Right or East Side

The barn door furthest to the right (east) provided access to the stalls on the east side of the milking area. It also had a small opening in the top to allow a conveyor track to run through.

Outside, above this door on the right side of the barn, was a long round beam about 12 inches diameter that was positioned about 9 to 10 feet above ground level.

The beam ran horizontally for about 20 feet out from the door and was suspended from above by several 1-inch wire cables attached to the side of the barn.

The conveyor that carried the litter carrier from inside the barn, was attached to the bottom of the beam. The litter carrier was used for removal of manure from the milking area.

The beam had a rope attached to the outermost end to allow moving and positioning on a 180-degree radius from the door. There was a large pile of manure below it, when we arrived.

The second door on the east side, provided access to the stalls for the cows on the west side of the milking area and the three horse stalls.

Left or West Side

On the far-left side of the barn (west side) a single door would provide access to the chicken coop and box-stall area.

The Ends of the Barn

On each of the ends of the barn's ground level (east and west walls) was another man door with two windows on each side of those doors.

Back or North side of Barn

The north wall or back of the barn had only the large roll-up door in the centre and one small door in the north/east corner box stall. There were two access ramps from the ground level to the second level.

Windows

There were three windows at the back of the barn. Two windows were in the north/west corner and the third was under the east ramp to allow natural light into the milking equipment cleaning area.

Support Structure of Ground Floor

The lower level exterior of the barn was built from large concrete blocks about 12 inches long x 10 inches high x 8 inches thick.

These blocks along with the internal column and beam structure, supported the second floor. The lower section of the barn was about 12 feet high under the beams.

Ground Floor of the Barn

The ground floor was divided into three areas

Area 1 - was the Milking Area on the east side,

Area 2 - was the common area between 1 and 3

Area 3 - was the box stalls and chicken coop on the west side

THE DAIRY PROCESS ON OUR FARM

Milking 101 - June 1950 to 1955

The milking needed to be done twice a day. My dad would get up at 5:00AM for the early milking before travelling to his work, and do the evening milking when he got home around 5:30 – 6:00PM

Although weekends provided a break from his sales job, running a dairy farm was a 7 day a week commitment.

Area 1 – Milking Area

The milking area took up the east side of the lower part of the barn. It was completely separated from the rest of the barn with a wall from the front of the barn to the back.

There was an access door from the centre common area of the barn to the milking area about ¾ of the way back to the north wall.

Protruding into the common area and running along the back (north) wall was the cleaning area for the milking equipment.

It had an entrance from the common area and one from the milking area. It contained the cistern described earlier.

In it was an electric pump that supplied water to wash the milking equipment and to supply a large drinking trough immediately in front of the cleaning room.

The large concrete drinking trough in front of this cleaning room was 30 inches deep x 30 inches wide x 10 feet long and was dated 1914.

The pump also supplied water to a large steel container fastened to the ceiling in the milking area.

This container gravity fed the individual stalls providing water to the cows.

Drinking Bowl

The cows would push down on the centre portion to release the water into the bowl. Sample bowl shown would normally connect to a water supply pipe

Next to the access-walkway to the cleaning room, was a small box stall. Next to it was a stairway to the second level of the barn where the hay and straw was stored. Finally, we come to a large box stall in the north-east corner.

The middle area contained the stalls where the cows were milked.

In the south west corner of the milking area, there were three horse stalls. Horses entered the stalls from the milking area and were fed from the common area.

AREA 1 -MILKING AREA JUNE 1950

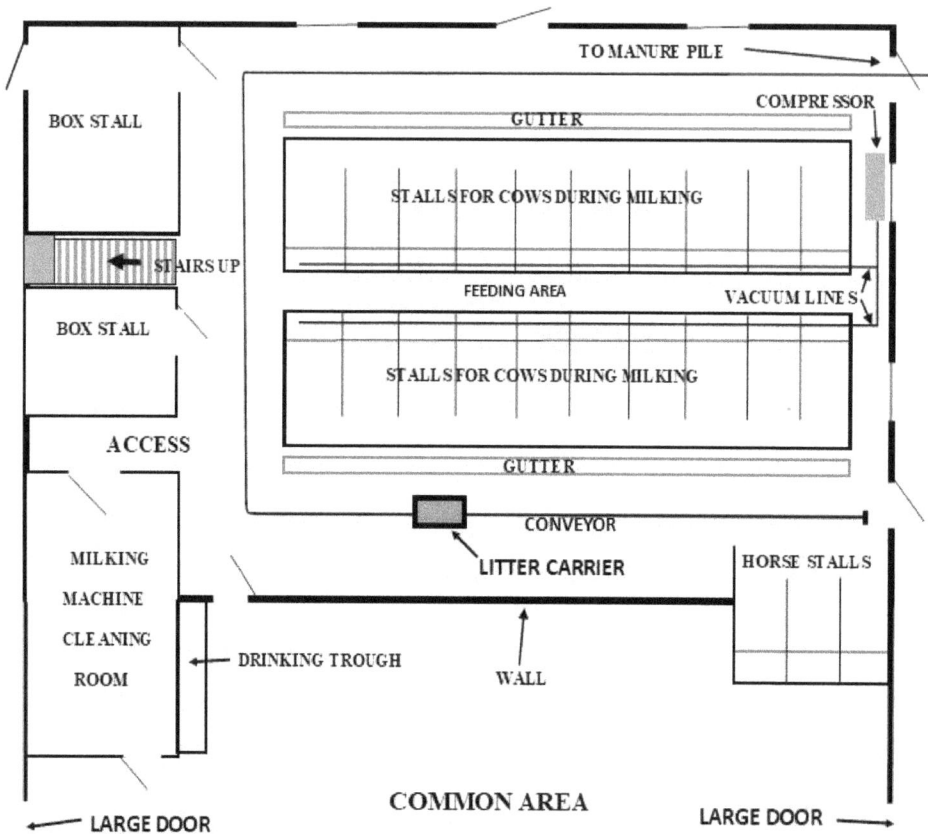

The Milking Area Description

The milking area itself consisted of two rows of stalls, a ten-foot-wide walkway on the outside of each row of stalls and the gutter for collecting the manure.

Between the two rows of stalls in the middle was the feeding area. This is where the hay was put down from upstairs for feeding, and straw for bedding.

The cows faced inward with a manger in front of them to allow for easy feeding.

Feeding the cows Hay

Each morning and evening in the months when the cows were not grazing in the fields, Brian and I would feed them hay and provide fresh straw for bedding.

Our Milking Process June 1950 to 1955

At the south end was a large compressor/vacuum pump. Connected to it, were two air lines running down the length of the stalls.

The lines provided individual off/on valve connections for each stall to operate the milking machines.

The milking equipment comprised of a small stainless-steel pail with removably top secured with wing nuts. There was a handle for carrying and cradle to hold the four-part milking attachment.

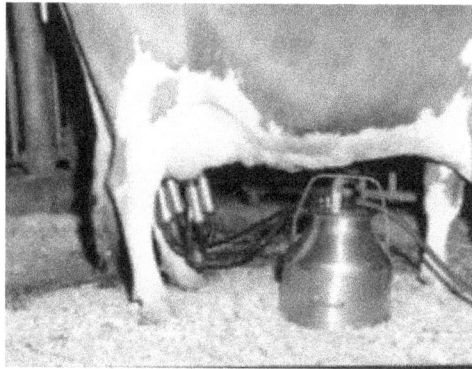

Milking Machine attached to Cow

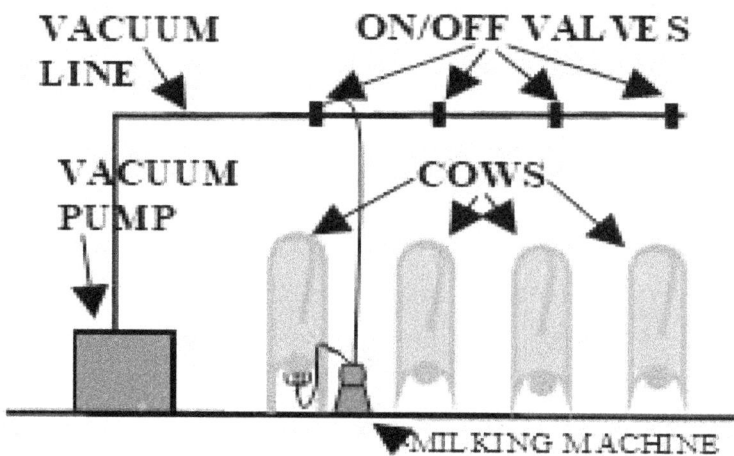

The System

How it Worked

A braided hose connected the pail to the air line and operated on a vacuum basis. The four pieces of the milking machine were attached to the cow.

Each of the four attachments had two parts (a stainless steel outer part and a rubber inner part). The pulsing vacuum action caused the inner section to squeeze the milk from the cow and the vacuum would pull the milk into the pail.

At the end of the mechanical milking part, it was necessary to complete the milking process by hand to make sure all the milk was removed to avoid infection. This process was called stripping.

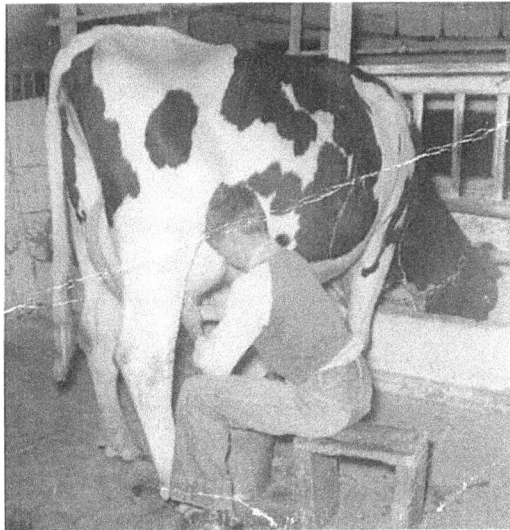

Me at age 10
Stripping the milk from a cow

After each cow was milked, the contents of the pail were poured through a filter into a milk can. When full, the can was taken to the cooler in the milk house to keep it cool until shipping.

Pouring and Filtering   **The Inground Cooler**

Under the ramp at the back of the barn on the west side, was where the milk house with its in-floor cooler was located.

Getting the Cows

In the morning and evening, it became one of our chores to bring in the cows for milking during the months when they were grazing.

We would walk or ride our bikes out to where the cows were pasturing, to bring them in. Our dogs Lassie and Laddie would help.

It was often made easy because the cows were habitual and would start their journey to the barn on their own or upon hearing our call *"Coe Bass, Coe Bass."*

I never knew why they responded to that phrase, but it worked. As soon as one or two began the journey, the rest would usually follow, often in a single line.

When entering the barn, they would go right to the stall designated for them. A chain was loosely put around their neck to keep them in place until the milking was done.

During the late spring, summer and early fall months when there was growth on the fields, the cows were released after milking.

They would return to the pasture area, to eat the grass in the fields. In the late fall, winter and early spring they remained in the barn, and were fed hay that we brought in during the summer.

Our Cows (Picture by Me)

CLEANING THE GUTTERS

The Gutters

Along the back of each row of cows, in the concrete floor, was an 18-inch-wide x 8-inch-deep trough or gutter to collect the manure.

GUTTERS IN FLOOR

Above the gutter and fastened to the ceiling, was a conveyor track that carried a large bucket (litter carrier). The litter carrier was about 24 inches wide x 30 inches deep x 48 inches long and could travel behind the stalls to gather the manure.

The Litter Carrier

The litter carrier could be lowered to allow easier cleaning. Once the litter carrier was full, it would then be taken outside.

The south/east barn door would be opened, and the litter carrier travelled along conveyor attached to the long boom to the desired location.

Here it was tripped, and the contents were dumped onto the ground below or into the manure spreader if it was there.

Spreading Manure

The area for this was called the manure pile and continued to grow until winter when the manure was removed and spread on the frozen fields. We would use the horse drawn manure spreader shown above.

AREA 2 OF THE BARN

Area 2 was located between areas 1 and 3. It was about 30 feet wide and ran from the front of the barn right through to the back.

There were two large roll-up access doors. They had an opening of 16 feet wide by 12 feet high. There was one on the south side, mirrored by one on the north side of the barn. They provided access for any larger equipment as well as access to areas 1 and 3.

Area 2 was a staging area for the animals (horses and calves) that were in the box stall area 3. The doors also provided access for removal of manure from the box stalls using an 8 to 12-pronged fork and wheel barrow.

The work horses and riding horse were all located in the south west corner of the milking area 1 but were fed from the common area.

Area 2 was also a play area for my brother Brian and me. We could ride our bikes here and play with our wagons as well.

The large doors provided a throughway for the milk cans to be taken to the milk house under the north/west ramp. Here they would be kept cold until they were later removed and transported to the front of the barn for shipment to the Dairy.

Each door operated on a counter weight basis to allow it to be opened easily. The door went straight up into a wooden enclosed shell in the upper portion of the barn.

Two one-inch diameter ropes were attached to the top of the door on each side and went up over wooden pulleys and down to be connected to the ends of a large beam. (The counter weight) Occasionally the rope would jump the pulley we would need to go in from the top to reset them.

Layout Description Area 3

The west side of the barn at ground level consisted of 8 large box stalls a 6-foot isle, a chicken coop and a storage area. There were 4 box stalls on the north side and 4 on the south side with an 8-foot-wide isle running east-west between them.

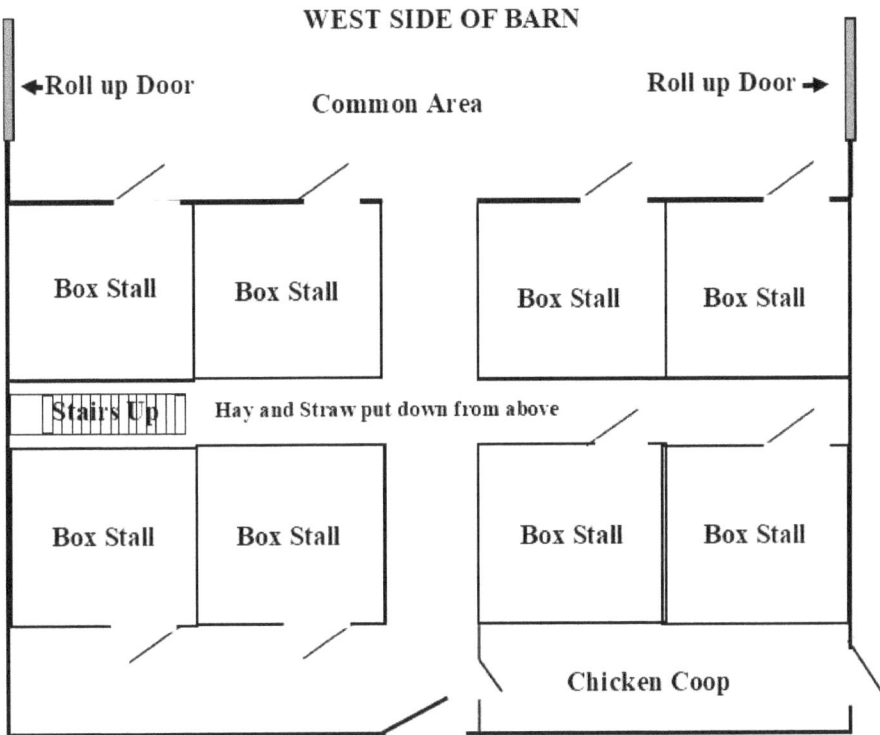

WEST SIDE OF BARN

Layout Area 3 at June 1950

The 4 inner stalls were accessed from the common area. Two stalls were accessed from the 6-foot isle running south to north and 2 stalls were accessed from the west side.

The side door also provided access from outside on the west side.

Construction

The lower part of the stalls was 48 inches high and constructed of a series of vertical 1 inch thick by 6-inch-wide tongue and grove boards.

The tongue and grove sections were capped by a 2-inch x 4-inch wood top, which also acted as a base for the upper section.

The upper section was made up of 48-inch-long spindles installed in an upright (vertical) position. They were made from 2-inch square wood with the corners shaved, to create 8 equal sides.

The spindles were inserted vertically into the 2-inch x 4-inch base and capped with another 2 by 4-inch beam at the top.

The overall box stall height was approximately 98 inches, leaving approximately 44 inches of clear open space above.

Two openings or chutes were located above the six-foot isle that ran south to north. They would allow hay and straw to be put down from the upper level.

There were several horses being boarded when we took over operations and we would continue to do this. One of the horses was black and named Pepper. We could ride this horse to keep it exercised.

On the south/west corner was the chicken coop. It was home to about 12 laying hens and one rooster on the day of our arrival.

SECOND LEVEL OF BARN

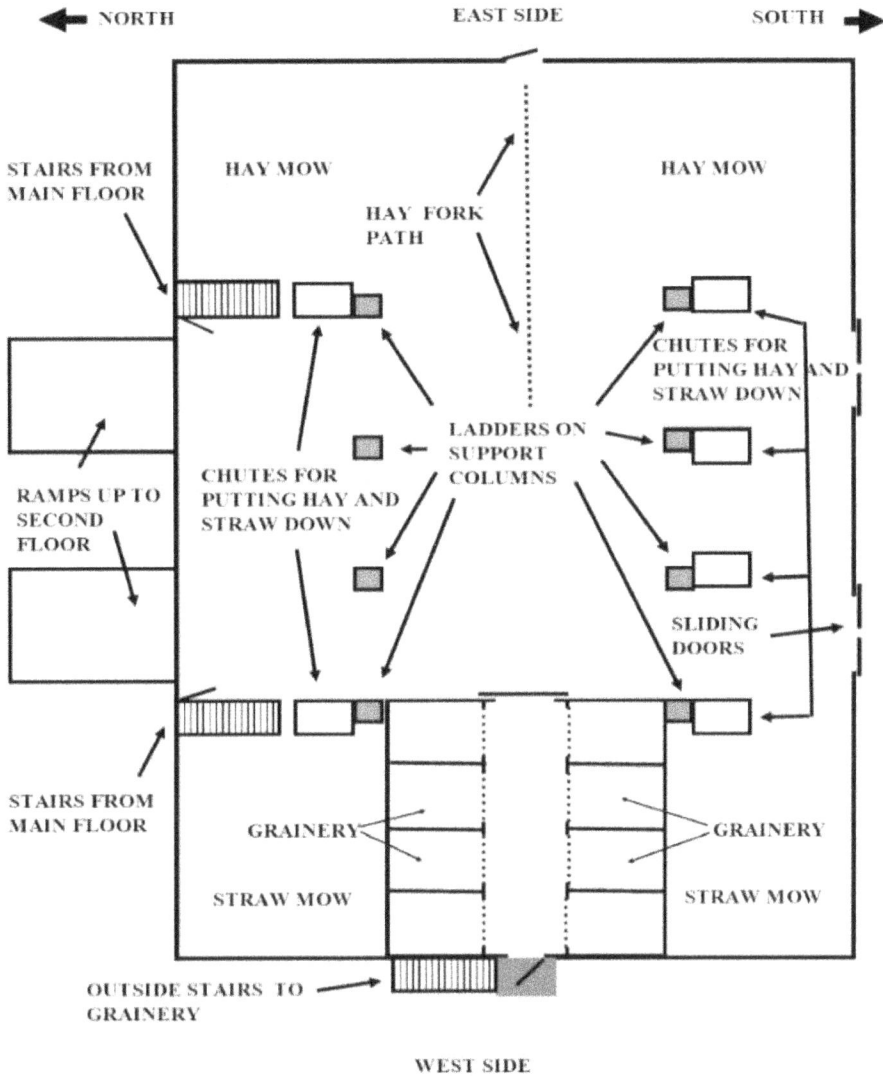

← NORTH   EAST SIDE   SOUTH →

STAIRS FROM
MAIN FLOOR

HAY MOW

HAY MOW

HAY FORK
PATH

CHUTES FOR
PUTTING HAY AND
STRAW DOWN

LADDERS ON
SUPPORT
COLUMNS

RAMPS UP TO
SECOND
FLOOR

CHUTES FOR
PUTTING HAY AND
STRAW DOWN

SLIDING
DOORS

STAIRS FROM
MAIN FLOOR

GRAINERY

GRAINERY

STRAW MOW

STRAW MOW

OUTSIDE STAIRS TO
GRAINERY

WEST SIDE

Support Structure

The main internal support structure for the walls and roof above the second floor, would be made from 16 to 18-inch square hand-hewn columns (posts) and similar sized support beams. The cross bracing from columns to beams would be 6-inch x 6-inch also hand hewn.

The floor of the second level, was made from large 4-inch-thick by 14 to 16-inch-wide planks and they were about 12 to 16 feet long.

The second level (second floor) had a clear height of about 30 feet to store the hay and straw before the roof started to angle in. The roof was in two parts, the lower roof and the peak roof.

Hay Mow

The main area for the hay mow was the entire upper east end of the barn. The wagons of hay would travel up the east ramp and into the central area immediately in front of the mow.

Starting with no hay in the barn, we would push the wagon manually into the centre of the east end and throw the hay off the wagon to each side south and north.

Ladders

The ladders were used to gain access to the hay mow when it was filling and full. They were all about 25 feet high.

The large upright 14-inch o 16-inch support columns were used for one side of the ladder and 6-inch x 6-inch square columns were used on the other side.

Eight-sided wood spindles (like the horse stall uprights) ran horizontally between the two columns and were used as rungs to climb up to the desired level.

Putting Hay Down

After throwing hay down from the hay mow, the chutes at floor level, were used to put the hay further down to the milking area to feed the cows.

The chutes were hinged at the top and free at floor level. They opened inward, allowing us to push hay in and down through the 40-inch-wide opening in the floor.

The Grainery

The grainery was 20 feet wide x 10 feet high x 40 feet long and was divided into eight sections or bins inside. There were four bins on the south side and four on the north side with an access isle in the centre.

At the front of each section (bin) were slotted sides. We would insert a one-inch thick x 8 inches high board to hold the grain in. As the grain level increased, more boards were added.

A man-door c/w stairs and landing provided access from outside. At the other end of the grainery, inside and on the second floor of the barn, was a 10-foot-wide sliding door to provide access to the wide isle between the two sides.

The Straw Mow

During threshing the straw was blown in to the west end of the barn and would fill the areas in the south and north sides of the grainery as well as on top.

Farm Layout on Move-In Day

FARM LAYOUT 1950

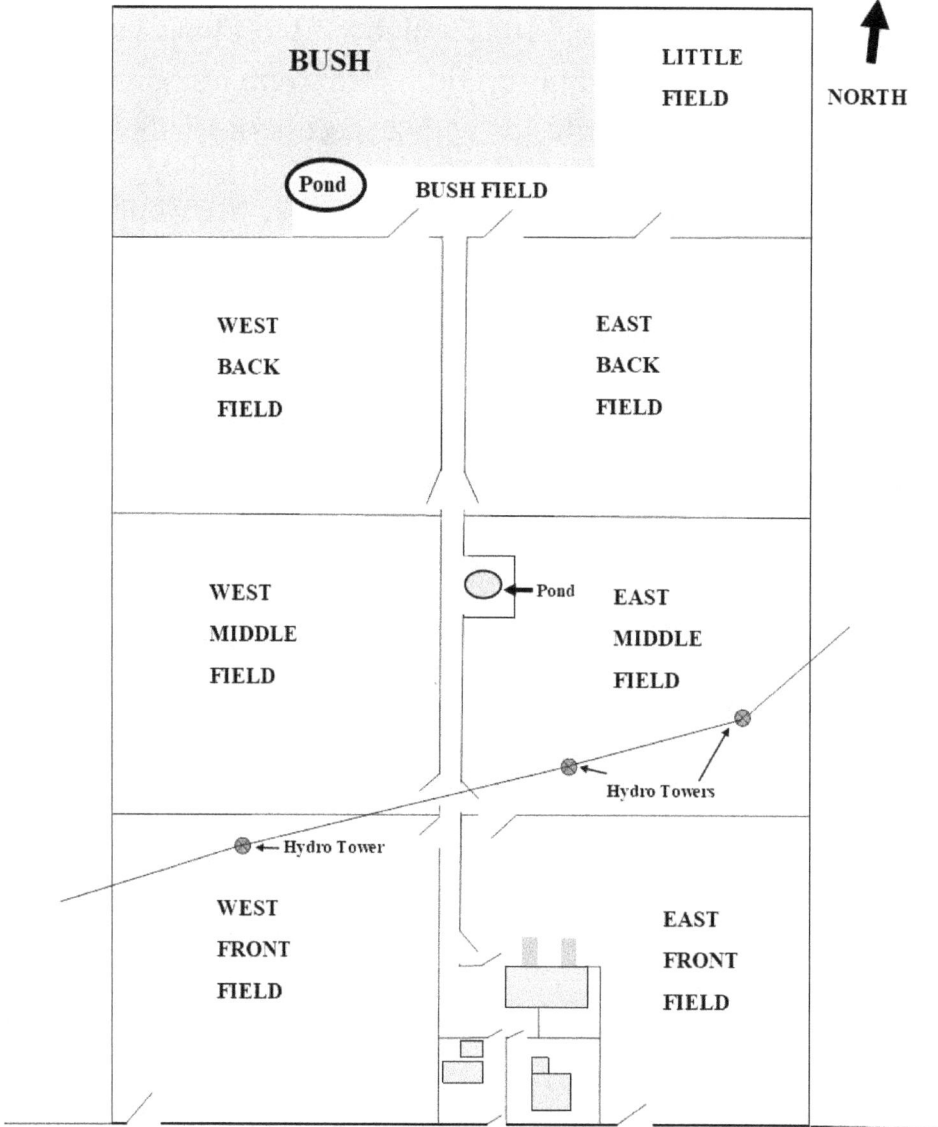

Farm layout diagram showing: BUSH, LITTLE FIELD, Pond, BUSH FIELD, WEST BACK FIELD, EAST BACK FIELD, WEST MIDDLE FIELD, EAST MIDDLE FIELD, Pond, Hydro Towers, Hydro Tower, WEST FRONT FIELD, EAST FRONT FIELD. NORTH arrow points up.

BACK CONCESSION– renamed BURNHAMTHORPE 1967

The fields would remain the same except for the West Front Field. In 1953, we would install a large pond in its south/east corner. We would also create a recreational area between the pond and house.

The farm was divided in halves by a laneway running northward from the barnyard area. It ran all the way back to the bush field in front of a 16-acre bush at the back of the farm.

There were three large fields per side, and a small six-acre field on the east side of the bush that we called the little field. There was a smaller narrow field in front of the bush. We called it the bush field.

Each field access point or opening was referred to as a gap. It had a loose wire gate to open the access or close it. There were about four strands of barb wire equally spaced attached to small vertical wood posts. They kept the gate upright.

One end of the wire gate was fixed, and the other end could be swung 180 degrees in either direction, to open or close the gap.

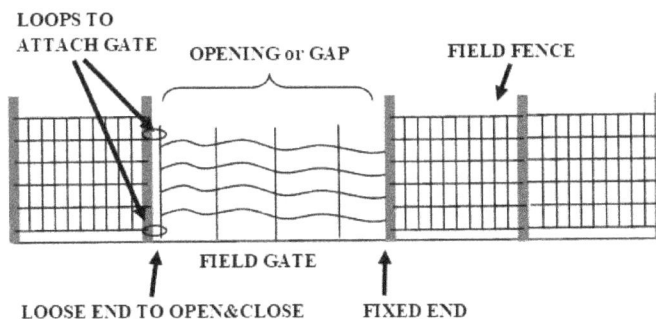

A Typical Gap

Closure of the gap would be achieved by inserting the bottom of the post on the loose end into a wire loop at the bottom of the stationary fence. A similar wire loop was brought down over the top of the post.

The Laneway

The laneway started on the west side of the equipment staging area west of the barnyard.

It ran from the staging area for about 30 feet westward and then turned north. It would run straight north to the bush at the back of the property.

The Pastures

Usually the laneway, bush field and the six-acre field beside the bush were set aside for pasture and the cows could travel down the lane after each milking to access them.

Once the crops on the hay or grain fields were in the barn these fields could also become pasture. Often there would be 2 crops of hay harvested per year, which meant they were not available for pasture until after the second crop was in the barn.

The Fields

On each side of the fenced-in lane, were the fields also totally enclosed by fences. There were three large fields on each side of the laneway with the barb-wire gates strung across the opening.

They were kept closed except when we were working the land, accessing the crops or being used for pasture.

These larger fields would be designated east front, east middle, east back, west front, west middle, and west back. At the back of the property in front of the bush running east from the lane was a narrow field. It was called the bush field.

To the right (east side) of the bush was a small six-acre field that we called "the little field".

In later years, we would use electric fences to further divide the fields being used for pasture, to create more efficient use.

The Official Shillum Drink

Work in the fields from spring until fall would see us with a jug or thermos of **Vinegar and Honey**. It would quench our thirst and provide energy.

It was always parked under a tree somewhere in the shade along with our lunch. Lunchtime was spent there, and usually did not involve returning from the field to eat.

For a break from the sun, lunch or a snack, we would unhitch the horses and let them graze in the shade while we stretched out under a tree. Often our spot would be under an apple or pear tree and it would provide dessert.

In the beginning, all operations were horse driven as we had no tractors when starting our farming experience. We did it the old fashion way. We would begin to add the use of tractors and tractor driven equipment in the third year.

We will describe the process using the horses as it was the most exciting part of being a young farm boy from the city.

The Attachments and Harnesses

The harnesses for the horses included an over the head bridal with a mouth piece called a bit. The bit was connected on each side to reigns that were used to stop and steer the horse. The collar, girth and trace or tug, were placed on the horse and connected to the equipment with the attachments below.

The Equipment Attachments

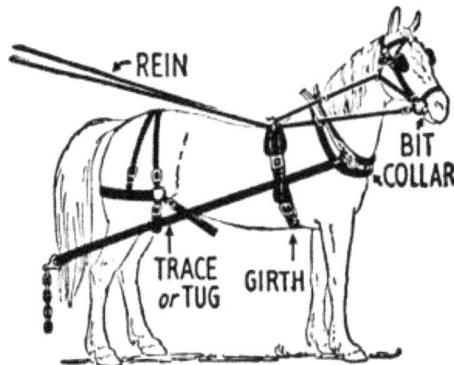

Harness Equipment

The collar, girth and trace were connected in line on each side of the horse to a wooden singletree that was attached to the equipment. For two horses they were attached by a double tree.

Attachments of Horse to equipment

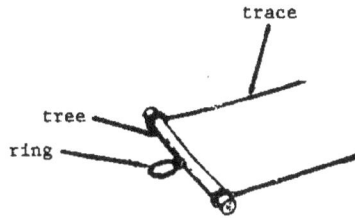

Singletree

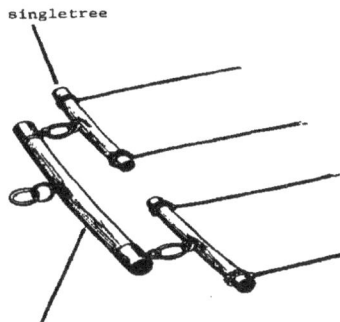

Doubletree

Controlling Movement and Direction

We had two very large work horses named Frank and Lauddie. I still remember the process of starting, stopping, steering, and backing up.

We would say **giddy up**, slap the reins up and down on their back and make a chucking noise to get things moving.

To steer right we would pull on the rein of the right horse while leaving the other loose. A verbal command for right was **"Gee"**. Turning left would involve pulling on the left rein, loosening the right one and yelling **"Haw"**.

Stopping was accomplished by pulling back on all four of the reins and yelling **"Whoa"**.

Backing up would involve pulling harder back on the reins and yelling the command **"Back"**.

These instructions would also be used when riding our horse trigger. The horses were trained to follow all verbal commands and the physical part was not a painful process for them.

Our horses Frank and Laudie

I am in the middle holding the Horses

On the right is Mrs. Taylor who was our Toronto

Baby Sitter

She is holding my brother Brian

On the Left is the son of our baby sitter Bill

In the background is the old drive shed that would be torn down

In the Spring of 1951

How We Did the Farm Work in 1950

Haying

We will describe the farm activities as we undertook them. We had arrived in the middle of haying season. We would be bringing in loose hay from the fields.

It would be a five-part process.

1-Cutting with horses and mower,

2-Curing – Nature took care of this,

3-Raking into rows with a side rake and horses,

4-Bringing it in with horses and wagon,

5-Putting it into the hay mow of the barn with horses.

Part One Cutting

We used our team of horses Frank and Laudie to pull the equipment. The device for cutting was called a mower.

It consisted of a steel frame with a wooden tongue to attach the horses. The mower had a steel seat to sit on and the cutting system was on the right side. Fields were cut in a clock-wise manner.

There was a hand brake that locked the wheels when needed. Although the horses were obedient, they might move without being told to do so.

The Horse Drawn Mower

The Mower in Action

How the Mower Operated

There was a combination of gears that operated the mower using the turning of its main wire spoked wheels to drive the rest. There was a long cutting arm about 6 feet in length on the right side of the mower.

The cutting arm had multiple pointed triangular knife guards attached to it with upper and lower parts for the knife to run inside them. The front of the guard was pointed, directing the hay to the cutting action.

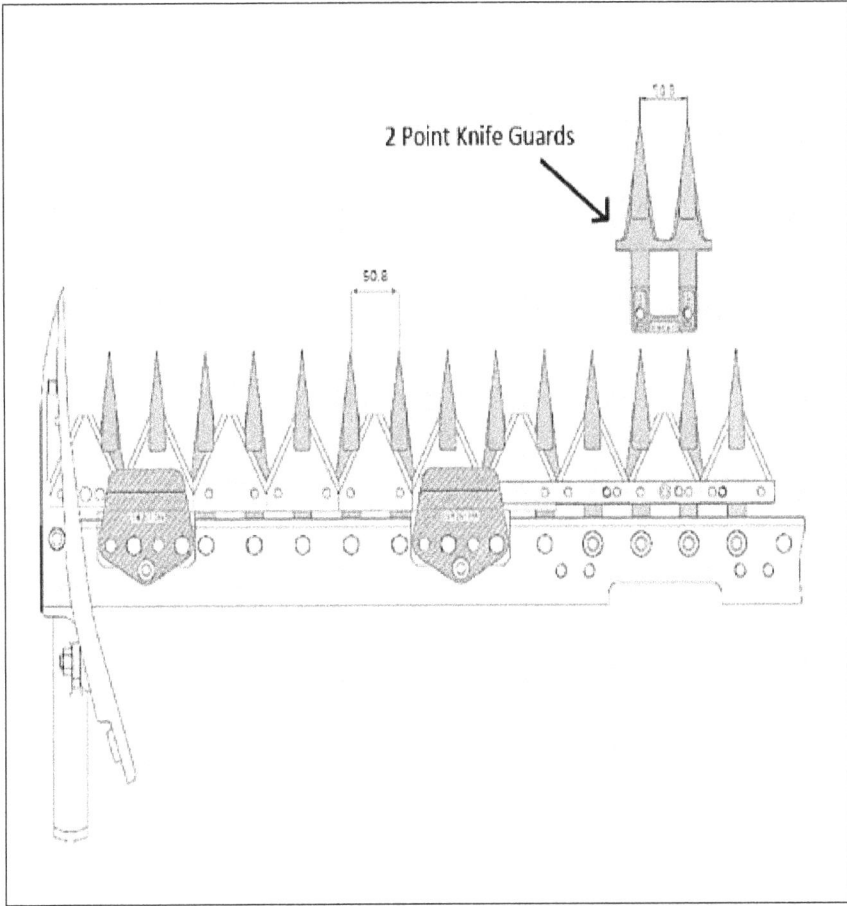

Above - Part view of cutting arm

How it Worked

The knife was made up of a series of 2-inch triangular blades. Two sides faced the oncoming hay and acted as the cutting edges. The third side was rivet attached at the back to a ¼ inch thick steel bar.

This bar would move back and forth created by the gear action of the wheels of the mower when turning. The steel clamps would hold the knife and blades in place while the hay was cut.

Both guards and blades were often damaged by rocks or fence wire and could be individually replaced when needed (which was often).

These spare parts were always kept close by, and repairs were most often made in the field.

When turning a corner, a lever would lift the six-foot cutting arm up about 8 inches off the ground. It was an acquired skill and took much practice to be perfected. The skill was required to avoid clogging the blades with already cut hay.

When not in use the gears would be disengaged from the long cutting device. The cutting arm would then be manually lifted and attached in a vertical position to the mower with a large wing nut.

We would watch my dad doing the field work from the edge of the field. During hay season, he alone would operate the horse driven mower to cut the hay.

I am not sure if my older brother Bob ever did, but I would never get the opportunity to cut hay with the horses.

Part 2 Curing

This part was easy as the summer breeze and the sun looked after the curing. The hay was left flat on the field after cutting for one to two days. Depending on weather conditions, it could be shorter or longer.

There was a sweet smell to the freshly cut hay that increased as the curing process took place. It was an aroma I still remember to this day.

In later years, and to this day; I will roll my car window down when passing a freshly cut hay field; when in the country, to catch a scent from my childhood days.

The Raking Equipment

The Dump-Rake

The dump rake was a process that was long and tedious. It involved dropping the wire prongs on the ground and gathering the hay to where a row of hay was or would be created.

Once you reached that location; a lever was pulled, and the prongs would rise leaving the gathered hay behind. We had the equipment but did not use the dump rake for putting the hay into rows. We used it to collect hay that had been missed by the hayloader.

The Side Rake

We would use a side-rake which was quicker and easier. It allowed raking into rows in a continuous action.

Part 4 - Bringing Hay in from the Fields

Bringing in the hay involved a horse driven wagon with a hayloader behind. In the beginning, and under close supervision, I would be allowed to take the reins and drive the wagon out to the field.

The Wagons

Wagons would range in size, but an average platform size might be 10 feet wide x 14 feet long. The front rack was the highest and might be 8 feet high with cross members to hold the hay in and to stand on when driving the horses as the load grew.

The rack at the back was slightly lower to allow the hay to enter the wagon from the hay loader. Our early wagon wheels were of a wire rimed wooden spoke design about 36 inches high.

Above - left to right is Brian, Mrs. Taylor and Me
Behind us is our Hay Wagon

Loading the Hay onto Wagon

The hay was now cured and in rows. It was time to collect the hay by using a hayloader. The horses were hitched up to a wagon with racks front and back to hold the loose hay.

A hay loader was previously taken to the appropriate field for its use. Upon arrival of the horses and wagon, the hay loader was attached to the back of the wagon.

The Hay Loader Attached to Wagons

There would most often be three people needed for this process. One to drive and two to distribute the hay and build the load.

Sometimes it was a two-person process which meant driving the team of horses much slower.

The driver would steer the horses so that there was one horse on each side of the loose hay on the ground, now in rows.

The wagon would travel above the row and the hay loader would pick it up behind the wagon and carry it up on a conveyor chute to the top where it fell into the wagon.

Another View loading the Hay

The people on the load would build the hay until it reached a height of 6 to 8 feet from the wagon surface. When the load was complete the hayloader was disconnected and we headed to the barn.

It would eventually become my job to drive the horses when collecting the hay.

Help from our Relatives

All my relatives lived in the city, so it would be a great adventure for them to come to the farm to take part in the haying.

One time I remember my Uncle Barney taking charge of driving the horses when collecting the hay. To him driving the horses looked easy, so he took over from me.

If I could do it at my age, certainly he could handle the task. Things were fine for a while until he dropped one of the rains and panicked.

His actions spooked the horses and they took off and literally buried my dad under the huge surge of hay that followed.

When the horses finally stopped, and we located my dad under the hay, my uncle resigned from his position as driver.

We enjoyed many laughs in the future, discussing his failed attempt.

Part 4 – Putting Hay into the Barn

The first years for me, would be mostly watching others, which included the unloading of the hay. There were two ramps at the back of the barn that led up into the upper level of the barn.

Looking south and facing the back of the barn, the left ramp (east) one was for hay and the right (west) one was for straw. Just inside each of the large doors on the second level of the barn were internal access doors from the ground floor inside the barn.

The access door from the milking area was on the left (east) side of the large entrance door of the east ramp. On the west side, and to the right (west side) of the large access door was the second stairway access from the box stall area below.

Up the Ramp into the Barn

Upon the return to the barn with the load of hay, the wagon was parked maybe 20 - 30 feet from the bottom of the ramp. The horses were given a short rest before starting up the ramp.

One person (my dad or older brother) would be the driver to take the load up into the barn. The others would proceed on foot separately up the ramp to the upper level first. They would provide some direction to allow safe passage through the doors.

This was always the breath holding part. Most of the time the trip up the ramp was without incident. There were rare times when the journey up and into the barn was not successful, and this meant backing down to safety.

This created the scary part as the driver would need to steer the horses back down the ramp while keeping the wagon from going over the edge.

Luckily there were only a few times when the wagon would go over the lower part of the ramp. Fortunately, the horses or driver were never injured when this happened.

Part 5a Unloading the Hay

The initial unloading and placing of the hay into the lower part of the hay loft at floor level, was done manually.

The horses were unhitched, and the wagon was manually backed into the middle of hay loft and unloaded and spread evenly on two sides by hand (using a 3-pronged pitch fork).

This was continued until the level on the two sides (north and south) reached about 6 to 8 feet in height.

When this manual process filled the two outer parts of the loft it was time to fill the centre area where the wagon had been positioned to fill the sides.

Part 5b The Hay Fork System

Once the wagon was in the upper part of the barn, the horses were unhitched and brought around to the top of the ramp where they were hitched to a double tree, rope and pulley system used to unload the hay.

At one end of the rope would be the team of horses. On the other end of the rope was the hay fork. A series of pulleys were between the two ends to guide the directional changes of the load of hay.

THE HAY FORK SYSTEM

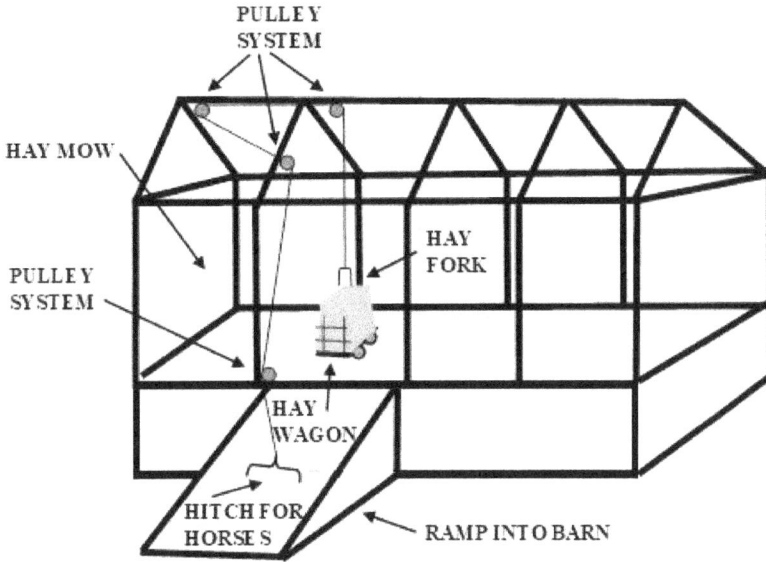

The two-pronged hay fork shown below, was used to lift the hay.

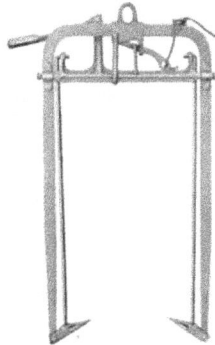

Hay Fork

At the bottom of the fork were two sharp ends. They would be manually pushed into the hay to the depth of the fork. A leaver on top was used to turn the ends of the fork inward at 90 degrees. It was locked to capture and secure the load to be lifted.

A second small rope was connected to the release part of the leaver, to allow the prongs to straighten. When the rope was pulled, it released the hay.

Unloading the Hay

Once the "all clear" was given the unloading process would begin. The horses were driven slowly down the ramp raising the load of hay to the top of the barn to connect with a set of wheels on the track.

Connector Wheels

The wheels were on a conveyor rail that ran to the back of the hay loft. The horses continued down the ramp pulling the fork and hay along the rail.

Releasing the Hay

Once the desired position was reached, the small rope was pulled to release and drop the hay. The horses were stopped, and they returned to the top of the ramp. The fork would be pulled back down manually, to lift another load.

Once all the hay from the wagon was in the mow, came the task of spreading it evenly until the centre part was higher than the two sides. At this point, we would manually spread the hay evenly to both sides, as the mow filled.

The Unloading with the fork system and spreading of hay would continue until the haying was done. The hay loft would often reach a height of 20 - 25 feet.

Although the fork process would be considered dangerous by today's standards, this was normal for haying in the early fifties.

Salting the Hay Mow

After each load, we would spread salt on the hay to make sure it cured and to prevent spontaneous combustion, which was the cause of many barns burning down.

Back Down the Ramp

Once the wagon was emptied, came another scary part of the exercise. We now had to hand push the wagon with one person steering it down the ramp. It was fine until the second set of wheels went over the edge of the barn floor.

There was no stopping it now as gravity took over. After that, it was up to the person steering, to direct it straight down the ramp. About half way down the person steering would have to drop the tongue of the wagon and hope for the best.

Once the wagon was safely at the bottom, it was time to hitch the horses to the wagon and get another load of hay.

More Help from Relatives

On one occasion, my cousin Russel was visiting. He came up the stairs to the hay loft from inside the barn.

He walked into the faces of the horses and driver waiting for the "all clear" to start down the ramp.

My cousin panicked, yelled and began running down the ramp. His sudden appearance, yell and running caused the team of horses to follow him.

This happened just as my older brother Bob was inserting the fork. He was standing on the fork and was suddenly travelling upwards.

Just before hitting the top; and experiencing a ride to the back of the barn, he jumped down onto the load of hay below.

The horses followed my cousin around the barn until the rope connection abruptly stopped them. The hay fork travelled to the end of the rail and jumped the track. My cousin kept running.

Although we would later laugh about this and tease my cousin for many years to follow, we were very lucky that my brother was not seriously injured or killed that day.

Threshing/Harvesting 1950 to 1953

After haying came the harvesting of our grain crops which meant relying on the community threshing system for the final part of this process.

The first part of the harvesting process would involve another horse drawn piece of equipment. It was called a binder.

Harvesting the Grain

Again, I would watch from the edge of the field while my dad operated the binder which cut the grain and tied it into sheaves.

I would join in the harvesting later when we put the sheaves into stooks (standing them upwards grain to the top and facing inwards in a circular fashion).

While similar in the design to the hay mower, it was a larger and more complicated piece of equipment.

Harvesting the grain was a four-part process:

1- *Cutting and binding the grain into sheaves,*

2 – *Stooking the sheaves,*

3 - *Bringing in the Sheaves*

4 - *Threshing.*

Part 1 - Cutting and Binding into Sheaves

The horses were still hitched to the front by a tongue and double-tree hitch system and the driver still sat on a steel seat. The entire process was driven by the movement of the equipment and gear system attached to the wheels.

Creating the Sheaves

At the front of the equipment was a five to six-foot-wide horizontal paddle wheel type device. It was about eight feet in diameter; and as it turned, it would push the grain into the binder where it was first cut by a process like the hay mower.

After being cut, it would then travel on a leather belt conveyor system where it was pushed to one side and tied into what was called a sheave, for handling. It then travelled down a wire chute to the outer edge, and then dropped on the ground.

Making Sheaves with the Binder

Part 2 - Stooking

The second part of the harvest and preparation for threshing was called stooking. This was primarily to dry and cure the grain but was an important part of drying and curing the straw as well.

Rows of Sheaves being Stooked

Stooking was a manual process which was mostly done by hand or could involve the use of a three-pronged pitch fork.

The sheaves of grain were usually 30 to 40 inches long (depending on type of grain and yield) and 12 – 14 inches in diameter at the tied part in the middle.

The Stooking is Done in this Field
The sheaves were placed with the grain pointing up.

After the first two were stood leaning together, other sheaves were placed around it. The group of sheaves would form what was called a stook. Normally there would be 10 to 12 sheaves in a stook and it would be maybe 40 – 48 inches diameter at the bottom.

Often, we would have a race to see who could finish a row of stooking first. It was great fun and made the work easier.

The stooks would be small enough to allow some air movement through them. They would remain in the stook until fully cured and ready for threshing.

Part 3 - Bringing in the Sheaves

A Community Effort

Each farm in the group of farmers requiring threshing, helped each of the other farmers when it was their turn to thresh. The community effort had a pecking order.

Being new from the city, we were at the end of the list.

At age six, I was not part of our family's contribution as that was left to my older brother, father and mother. The first year I would look after my younger brother Brian.

Threshing Day

The threshing machine came the night before, for an early start. Threshing day was like nothing that a six-year-old city boy could imagine. The other farmers started arriving with their horses and wagons shortly after their milking chores were done.

Usually it was before the morning dew had left the ground. It was not only a work day, it was a social gathering.

The arrival of the horse drawn wagons was an event I will never forget. Upon their arrival, they were lined up to begin when the time was right. (when the dew was gone and the stooks were dry enough)

Before work began there was much hand shaking and back slapping and laughter. Some would quietly puff on their corn cob pipes.

Soon after the arrival of the wagons, came the wives and daughters to begin preparation of the mid-day lunch. The lunch was also something I will never forget.

Time to Start

Depending on the size of family or if one had hired hands there was usually 3 to 5 people per wagon. One would drive, one or two would load and one or two would build the load.

Loading the sheaves onto the wagons

I think the first year my dad hired someone to even up our contribution. Unfortunately for that person, he ended up with one of the dirtiest jobs. It would be either in the grainery, or spreading the straw in the mow as it was blown in.

Part 4 - Threshing

Threshing was the final part of the harvesting. It involved the separation of grain from the straw.

Threshing for our concession was dependent on one farmer **Henry Proud.** He owned the threshing machine, which he alone operated.

The Threshing Machine

I remember Henry because his job at each farm; including his own, was to run, watch, oil and grease the threshing equipment.

The equipment (threshing machine) was very large and was driven by a large pulley and belt connected to his tractor. There were a series of additional belt driven pulleys producing different operations in the machine.

Threshing in Operation

Henry would apply the belt dressing to keep the belts from slipping off the pulleys. He also maintained the proper tension on the main tractor/thresher belt for the same purpose.

He would squirt any of the children with his oil gun if they got too close. He was extremely accurate, so none of us ventured close enough to become a target.

Sometimes the perimeter would increase as he enjoyed the target practice immensely and would laugh when his shots were successful.

Into the Threshing Machine

The sheaves were thrown onto a conveyor belt at the front of the threshing machine, and it then carried the sheaves into the machine.

Throwing Sheaves onto the Conveyor Belt

Once inside, the twine was cut, and the grain was shaken until the grain was removed and separated. The grain was separated from the straw and blown into the grainery through a 6-8-inch diameter pipe.

It also could be bagged at the side of the machine. There were two sides to the bagging section, with a leaver to switch sides, when a bag was full.

Someone would remove the full bag of grain and put another empty bag in its place.

At one point I remember learning how to tie the bags of grain in a special way to prevent them from spilling out.

The straw was blown into barn through an 18 to 24-inch diameter stack at the end of the equipment and the spreading the straw was probably the dirtiest of all the jobs.

The process involved 7 people. Two loading the machine two in the grainery or bagging, and two spreading the straw in the barn, and of course Henry with the oil gun.

Lunch Time on Harvest Day

It was a sight to see. Tables stretched the length of our west lawn beside the house. We would bring out the wood table from the kitchen and add the extra leaves.

Usually additional tables were brought by others in the group, on the empty wagons, at the start of the day. The farmers also contributed beef, chicken, pork, and vegetables from their own livestock and gardens.

Homemade bread and rolls were stacked in abundance. What I remember the most were the deserts - the cakes, the tarts, and then the pies - apple, cherry, peach, raisin, blueberry, plum, lemon, custard, banana, and more.

It was a feast I will never forget. As a six-year old I did not sit at the main table with the adults but joined others my age at our own table.

The same thing happened at every farm and made threshing one of the most memorable, social and community events of the summer. Our crop was usually a one-day event and seemed to end all too quickly.

PREPARING THE LAND IN 1950

Part 1 - Fall Plowing

It seemed there was little time for a break before winter. No sooner was the threshing done and it was time to start preparing the land for our grain crops.

It was time to hitch the horses to the one-furrow plow and get the fields ready for the planting of fall wheat, or next year's grains.

The One Furrow Plow

For wheat, plowing needed to begin as soon as harvesting was finished and was immediately followed by discing and harrowing. The final part was the planting of the wheat.

For Oats and other grains, it still meant fall plowing, but the discing harrowing and planting would be done in the spring.

How the Plow Worked

The angled and pointed end of the plow would cut into the soil to the required depth 6 to 8 inches and turn the soil over so that the top was now on the bottom. The rows were called furrows.

Horses and Plow

There aroma of the freshly turned soil was a breath of new life, and of a new beginning. I do not know how the information was obtained, but shortly after plowing began, swarms of seagulls would appear.

They covered the fields eating the worms and grubs exposed by the plow.

Part 2 - Discing

This equipment comprised of large 12-16-inch diameter discs side by side perpendicular to the ground.

They were slightly conical in shape and would slice into the plowed surface and begin the break up.

There were two positions. One for travelling place to place where the discs were parallel to the direction of travel, and the other was the angled positions to cut into the soil which is shown in the picture below.

Horses Discing

Although the equipment was heavy we would often place rocks turned up during the plowing and discing process on top of frame of the discs.

It would enhance the cutting into the soil and its break-up, and further clear the field of rocks at the same time. There was a steel seat above the discs for the driver to operate the discs and steer the horses.

Part 3 - Harrowing

Once the discing was done, it was time for the harrowing. The harrows consisted of two to four sections with many spikes about six to eight inches in length.

The Equipment for final Preparation

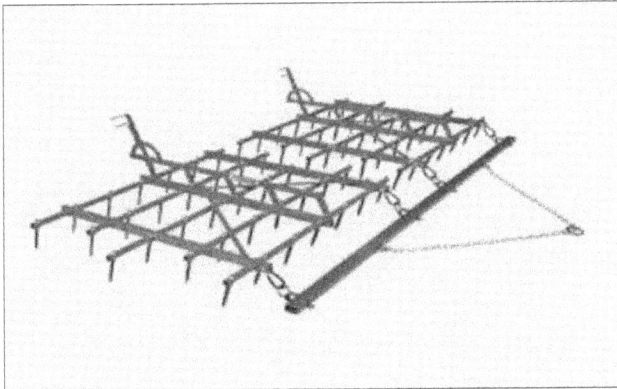

A Section of Horse drawn Harrows

Harrows in Action

How They Worked

The pointed spikes were about 6 to 8 inches long and positioned on 4 to 6-inch centres. The sharp end was pointed down ward.

The harrows could be increased or decreased in density or area covered, by hooking or unhooking the sections in two's. (One on each side) Often the driver would walk beside the harrows while holding onto the reigns and steering the horses if there was no seat.

The harrows were dragged over the disced surface, further breaking the soil into a fine powder-like consistency, in final preparation for planting (seeding).

Seeding

There were two times for planting grain, fall and spring. The grains we normally planted were oats and wheat and were annual plants.

Each planting was only good for one crop. For wheat, seeding was done in late summer or the fall. Harvesting would take place the next year in the summer.

Spring Planting (Seeding)

For spring planting, the fields would usually be plowed in the fall. Discing, harrowing and seeding would take place in the spring. Harvesting would take place in late summer of that same year.

Seeding Equipment

Another horse drawn piece of equipment would be used called a seed drill. It was on large 48-inch-high steel rimmed wooden wheels. The upper portion had boxes for seed. It stretched across the entire area to be seeded.

The Seed Drill Not in use

A large box would hold the grain, and a smaller box below would hold fertilizer or seeds for a future hay crop to germinate in the spring.

A Seed Drill in Operation

The openings could be adjusted for seed size.

The grain seed would fall down a flexible steel tube to a steel wedge shaped planter that would open the ground and allow the seed to be planted in the soil.

Hay seeds were perennial and took a full year to mature. Often hay seeds would be spread with a manual hand cranked seeder.

Fertilizing - Most often seeding and fertilizing were done together.

Culti-Packing

Often a final process was rolling the freshly planted soil with a culti-packer that would embed the seed into the ground for better yield and to minimize the loss from the gulls, starlings and crows that were always present during seeding.

Culti-packers

Field being Culti-packed

Rolling Alternative

Often a large roller filled with water was used to compact the soil instead of a culti-packer. It also was horse drawn, with or without a seat to sit on.

MY SUMMER OF 1950

My first summer on the farm was one of exploring. With 100 Acres as a back yard it was a far cry from the 50ft x 50ft yard in the city.

One memory that stands out, was racing down the ramps behind the barn with my brothers (mostly Bob, my older). We had two wagons and would position ourselves at the top of each of the two ramps.

Upon the signal, we would start our journey down. We spent hours and hours racing for many days that first summer and the ones to come.

Exploring the main barn and the equipment barns was an adventure viewing all the farm equipment. In the old garage, we found a Model T in working condition.

Although I was too young to drive, it did not stop my brother Bob from taking many trips up and down the lane that summer. We would ride as passengers.

I do not know what happened to the old car but looking back it was a rare find that would eventually have had considerable value.

My younger brother Brian and I were too young to ride our horse Trigger on our own that first year. Our older brother Bob, would enjoy many trips riding and exploring the farm that year.

We would get our turn, with Bob safely leading the horse.

There were many pictures taken of us and visitors sitting on Trigger that first summer and many summers to follow.

Yes, that's me

Mom, Mrs. Taylor, Me, Brian and Bob

Cousins Russel & Jack and me, Brian, Bob

-Dad, Trigger, Brian and me

View of west side of house
With me on Trigger

Mom, Bob, Brian Me

Two Families of Cousins
Bob, Russel, Me, Brian, Marilyn, Donald, Gary

Other Activities

We would also take long walks back the laneway that stretched all the way to the bush at the back of the farm. Along the fence line of the lane were many fruit trees and even grapes on the fences themselves.

At the beginning of the lane, there were several cherry trees, a plum tree and a pear tree.

Many sandwich lunches were packed along with our vinegar and honey drink for our adventure. It would be topped off with our choice of fruit desserts along the way.

When we reached the bush, I became Robin Hood with my very own Sherwood Forest to explore. I would lose many arrows in the bush and fields fighting the evil Sheriff of Nottingham and his solders.

I would always replenish my supply of arrows on our trips to Eatons in Toronto.

There were several mud holes in the lane where hundreds of white and yellow butterflies would gather after a rain. We would often head out after a rain to see the gathering.

We would make kites and spend hours flying them in the fields. We would have to do this away from the hydro lines and towers.

Evening Milking

It would become our daily chore to get the cows for evening milking. We would bring them as far as the barnyard and with the two barn doors open, they would go to their individual stalls on their own.

Magic Moments

I remember spending many evenings during the milking, lying in the hay between the two rows of milking stalls and watching the cows munch on their hay and enjoying their treats of chopped up grain.

I would watch the barn swallows as they nested between the beams above. They seemed to ignore our presence after their days outing.

I would occasionally sneak some molasses from the barrel located at one end of the space between the mangers, or chip pieces of salt from a large blue block beside it.

The block would eventually be taken to the pastures for the cows, but the molasses supply seamed to never end.

There was always something magical and peaceful during these times, and they will remain among my fondest memories of the early days on the farm.

Other Chores

There were so many chores that a six-year-old city boy could do, and I remember them well.

We only had around a dozen laying hens in the early days and they were truly free range as the door of the barn was usually left open for them to roam.

Although there were nests in the barn, we would come to know their favourite places to lay eggs outside. It was always a challenge and adventure to find the eggs each day.

The action of reaching under a chicken to get an egg, was most often met with a painful sharp peck on our hands. We used to grain feed the chickens every day along with some sort of small pellets to make the egg shells stronger.

There was a very small garden behind the house where we would collect potatoes, beans, carrots, and cucumbers. There were wild grapes, wild strawberries and raspberries along the east fence of the house.

Breakfast

This was one of the real family meals during the week when my dad was working in the city. We would all gather just as my dad was coming in from the morning milking session.

I remember toast piled up to what seemed like a foot high, with as many eggs and as much bacon and fried potatoes, as we wanted.

Milk was of course, always in abundance. In the early days we drank it unpasteurized; but later, my mom would do our own pasteurizing on the stove. It would never taste as good as the unpasteurized.

We used to have contests to see who could eat the most eggs or pieces of toast. My mom always had plenty of homemade jam at the breakfast table.

The good part about eating so much was that, there was no problem burning off the calories back then, with all our activities.

STARTING SCHOOL FALL 1950

The summer of 1950 was one to remember with so many great adventures of our new life on the farm. It seemed to end all too quickly. September finally arrived, and it was time to start school. At the age of six, I was in grade one and at 12 Bob was in grade seven.

My brother Bob and I would attend the one room school in Palermo that was located on the north side of highway 5 just east of Bronte Road (Hwy. 25).

The original school was built on the north side of Dundas Street in 1875. The building was ultimately destroyed when the roof was hit by lightning during a severe storm, and the building burned down.

The second Palermo school house was also built on the north side of Dundas in 1942, complete with the cornerstone of the previous schoolhouse, and was used as a school until the late 1950's.

Palermo Public School Built 1942

The picture is an early picture (probably about 1945) of how the front of the school looked with its double entrance doors.

Across the front was the wire fence c/w gate. There was access to the left on the west side for horses, or cars. This picture is very much as I remember it. The trees were larger in the 50's.

Back of school

A view of the back of the school. The small section on the right had the stairway we used to go down to the basement.

Upon arrival in good weather the back door was locked and would not be opened until just before classes would begin.

We would all leave our lunch pails along the back wall and wait for the bell which was the call to class. The teacher would appear at the back door and swing the hand-held bell up and down to signal class was about to start.

With the signal of the bell, we would then line up in two rows (girls left side, boys on the right) and proceed down the stairs into the basement.

There was one cloak room on the right (west side) for boys and one on the left (east side) for the girls.

Here we stored our lunches and jackets in our separate cloak-room/wash room.

In each cloak room, there were wooden peg coat hangers and a shelf above to place your lunch pail. On the floor under the coat pegs were wooden benches to sit on while we removed our rubber boots or winter boots.

The two large cloak rooms were separated by the stairway up. Half way up these stairs was the front door for the main visitor access in and out of the school.

Inside the Classroom

The above picture shows the blackboards that stretched across the entire room. Each Grade would be allotted space for the subject of the day and for spelling and arithmetic solving.

The blackboards stretched across the entire room. Each Grade would be allotted space for their activities. Grade one started on the right side (facing north and blackboards), and grade 8 was on the far-left side.

In the south west corner of the classroom was a stool with a dunce hat sitting on it.

One would wear it when being punished; mostly for not getting homework done. I would wear it on many occasions.

On the south/west side just beyond the classroom was the nurses room while on the south/east side was the teachers room. Between the two were the stairs that came up from the basement and front entrance.

A Typical School Day

Our school day would start with the Lord's Prayer and singing of God save the King.

This was followed by the singing of a hymn chosen by one of the students. Then came announcements by the teacher followed by current events provided by any student who had interesting news.

This news often included the birth of kittens, puppies a new born calf (baby cow) or colt (baby horse).

Out teacher Mrs. Wettlaufer would teach one grade at a time after giving the others their assignments that were written on the board. A second teacher was later added to handle the increasing enrolment.

Schoolyard

The Schoolyard Play Area

We would have a 30-minute morning recess, a 60-minute lunch and a 30-minute afternoon recess.

Both sides and back of the schoolyard were enclosed by the same type of wire fence as seen in the picture of the front of the school. Right behind the school was home plate and the baseball diamond.

Right field was slightly interrupted by a well and large hand pump.

Further down the right side, about half way back; just inside the fence, was the remains of a stone wall. We would use this fort-like recessed area to play our war games.

On the left side of the lot and part way back was another chestnut tree with a swing. It was not in the direct play zone for baseball. Usually if you hit the ball that far, it was a home run.

Summer Games

Chestnut Wars

By the time I attended the school in 1950, the chestnut trees along the front and both sides of the school had grown considerably from the picture.

They would yield our main components for the chestnut wars. We would eagerly select the largest chestnuts to take home and cure in the oven in preparation for battle.

"Chestnut Wars" used a bake-hardened chestnut. If you were caught short, you might try to use one just out of the shell on a string, but they usually had a very short life.

We would make a hole in the middle of the baked chestnut allowing us to put a string through it. At the bottom end we tied a large knot to keep the chestnut on the string. (shoelaces were best)

It was a very difficult process to make the edge of the hole free of cracks that would lead to early defeat. Most of us had very sharp jack knives to create nice clean edges. (they were allowed in those days)

The war consisted of swinging your chestnut and hitting your opponents to break it or knock it off the string. The opponent would dangle their chestnut vertically while you took your turn.

A turn would allow you to hit your opponent's chestnut once. It would then be the opponent's turn to hit yours. One would gain points (years) for each opponent's chestnut destroyed.

The person with the most accumulated years at the end of the day or week, would win.

Baseball

At each break, there was a mad rush to the baseball diamond to secure one's spot in the batting order by stepping on home plate.

The claiming order was first up, second up, third up, (fourth up), catcher, pitcher, first base, second base, third base, short stop, first field, second field and so on, until we ran out of people.

A batter would keep their position until they got out. With each out people would move one position closer to the "at bat spot".

If someone caught a fly ball, they would replace the batter by exchanging positions. No one advanced.

We would also pick teams and play against each other. This was usually an all-day game. Here the rules were like normal baseball.

Red Rover

I remember "red rover" where teams were picked, and we lined up opposite each other in two rows, about 15 - 20 feet apart.

We stood in our line with tightly held hands. Tightly was needed to prevent anyone from breaking through.

I liked this game as it presented the opportunity to hold hands with a girl I liked without obvious overtones and teasing. Sometimes there was a scramble to be next to a popular girl.

One team would call "red rover, red rover let (their choice) come over". The object of the game was for the person chosen, to break through their opponent's line somewhere.

If you did break through, you were a hero and returned to your position on your old team.

If you did not break through, you joined the opposition and went to one of the ends of their line. The game continued until one side had only one or two people remaining.

Marbles

Marbles was another very competitive game. As one's bag of marbles grew from the winnings, you would cherish your newly acquired collection of cat's eyes, clear, clay and other sought-after types.

Closest to the Wall

We would use marbles or sometimes pennies and see who could throw their item to end up closes to the wall. The closest would win and collect the entries from all other competitors. With pennies, a leaner took all.

School Christmas Preparation

During the late fall, the whole school would travel many times down the sidewalks on the north side of Dundas, cross at the intersection and travel to our destination, the community hall in Palermo. We would spend half a day or more practicing for the Christmas Concert.

It was great fun and the announcement of the planned activity, was always greeted with much enthusiasm – often cheering.

The Community Hall

At Christmas, the school would put on a play in the Community Hall and provide additional entertainment for the whole community with our singing of Christmas carols, piano playing or fiddling. Santa would pay a visit and provide toys for all of us.

Winter Games

There would be skating and hockey games on the river (14-mile creek) beside the school (east side) once it was safe. We would often return from our recess or lunch breaks with soakers and very cold feet.

We would all string our wet clothing on makeshift racks in front of the open furnace door in the basement. Here we would dry our socks, hats, scarfs and rubber boots.

In the school yard, there would be the building of snowmen and competitions for the best or biggest. We would build snow forts and have great snowball fights which often ended with a full-scale charge and trampling the opponents fort.

This was usually followed by washing their faces with snow.

In the colder weather or rainy days, we would have lunch in the basement. We would often open the furnace door and toast our sandwiches over the hot coals. Often someone would bring marshmallows.

Another popular winter pass time for both boys and girls alike, would be knitting and crocheting. We would trade yarn and see who could make the longest scarf or best pot holder.

In the spring, we would sail make-shift boats down the river beside the school.

Summer would once again see many of the older boys leaving school early, to help with the beginning of haying season. This was a normal and accepted practice in those days as a rural community.

School Bully

One event that stands out, was my confronting of the school bully. After continued harassment that was inflicted on all the students, one day I had had enough.

Victor was in grade three at the time and I was in Grade two. I confronted Victor and a full-blown fight took place. Although he was much larger than me, I managed to beat the pulp out of him.

I think he would bully everyone because of his size, and everyone was totally intimidated. It was probably the first time anyone stood up to him. After the fight, we became best friends and the bullying stopped.

Graduation

Each year our school commencement would also be held in the community hall where the Christmas concert had been.

Graduation Picture Class of 1950/51

My brother Bob is the tall one in the back row
I am 4th from the left in the front row

Another Class Picture
I am first from the left in the front row

Here I am holding the small Blackboard

We had no buses to take us to and from the one-room school, so it became a shared process where my dad most often picked up three of our neighbours and drove us all to school and one of our neighbours drove us all home.

By the fifth grade I would have a bicycle and make the mile and a half journey to and from school, weather permitting.

CHANGES TO COME

Bob would graduate in 1952 and attend (OTHS) Oakville Trafalgar High School. He would go on to graduate from Oakville Trafalgar.

Palermo Public #3

About 1956 the old one-room school would fade into history with the building of a four-room modern public school. It brought more students as other rural schools were also closing. I would finish grade 8 of public school at Palermo

ATTENDING CHURCH IN PALERMO 1950s

Front View St. Lukes Anglican Church

Above, is the Palermo St. Lukes Anglican church that we would attend. To the right of it, is a partial view of the parish hall. This is very much how I remember it. My mother was the primary figure in our family when it came to religious matters.

Seating for the Shillum Family

Just like threshing, there was a pecking order for where you could sit. We were relegated to the second pew from the back on the far-right side. There would be no one behind us for a while, except for the occasional visitors.

It was probably the best location for us as my dad would often fall asleep and start snoring during the sermon. My mom would shake him, and everyone would laugh including the minister.

The minister would often make a comment directed at my dad, at the beginning of his sermon asking him to try and stay awake.

My dad took in good humour and gave his full attention unless it was too long or boring.

Harvest Sunday

This day was something special to a farming community. We would arrive the first year and every year after, to an unbelievable display of every type of hay, grain, vegetable and fruit one could imagine.

The display would take up the entire front of the church. It was the product of Mr. Atkins Senior, and something to look forward to each year. Of course, one of the songs we would sing was: *"Bringing in the Sheaves"*.

Christmas Decorations

The same effort was made by Mr. Atkins Sr. at Christmas, as the front of the church was once again decorated for the season at hand. There would be a manger, and figurines of Mary, Joseph, Jesus and the three wise men and a few animals.

There was always a large decorated Pine Christmas tree and pine and cedar branches with decorations everywhere. Each pew had a display of pine cones, holly and ivy on each end of it c/w a red bow.

The Christmas Concert

We would also attend the Christmas concert in the parish hall beside the church. There would be entertainment and all the home-baked Christmas treats you could possibly eat.

There would be a lot of singing, solos, duets, the church choir and then everyone. There was usually a play "the arrival of the three wise men", and the singing of: "we three kings".

There would be the reciting of the *"Christmas Story"* (verses from the bible) and *"The night before Christmas."* There were piano solos and duets, fiddling and even Christmas songs from an accordion.

The first year we were just spectators except for the eating and group singing. One of the group songs would be: *"The holly and the Ivy"*. Santa would finally arrive, and we would all get presents.

In later years, after joining the church choir, I would provide entertainment with a solo like "Good king Wenceslas".

Danny Pope and I would usually entertain with a duet.

Christmas Parties at the Atkins

Each year one of the church members *George Atkins Jr.* would hold an *"all day"* Christmas party with sleigh rides, skating and even a bonfire and marshmallows.

Afterwards we would all come inside for hot chocolate and more Christmas treats and games. At the end Santa would arrive and we once again got presents.

These parties would continue for many years and were always an eagerly anticipated event and one of the highlights of the season.

Other Church Celebrations

In the Spring, there would be a service dedicated to the planting of the crops. The minister would bless a container of soil from some of the farms and seed for planting.

And then there was the "Strawberry Social". Once again, we would gather in the Parish hall for a feast of cake, strawberries and whipped cream.

The Parish hall would also become the meeting place for cubs and scouts where we would all work at obtaining our merit badges.

My New Duties

I sometimes think that my mother wanted me to become a minister as she encouraged (pressured) me into becoming a server in the church.

This meant that at every communion, I would assist the minister as he gave the communion offerings of bread and wine to the congregation. This lasted about 3 years until I finally had my say, and these duties ended.

Much to my mom's disappointment, I did not become a minister.

The Church Choir

Both my brother Brian and I would spend a brief time in the church choir.

**Brian and I rehearsing for the
Church Christmas Concert**

FARM MEMORIES OF 1950

Repair and Maintenance 1950

The farm was in a bad state of disrepair and it would take several years to bring it back to an acceptable level.

One of the first things my dad would tackle would be safety related areas. They would include repair and capping of the two outdoor wells by the house and replacing the access door to the cistern in the front shed.

In each of the three locations, water samples were taken at the start and tested for contamination. At the end the same tests would occur.

Well Number One

Removal of the old hand pump and rotting wood planks from the wells would reveal some shocking *"previously out of sight"* problems. The water level was approximately 7-10 feet below ground surface.

The Obstacles

The first things to encounter would be the nests of snakes under the rotting wood boards and in the upper portion of the well that was not under water.

After dealing with the snakes, came the removal of a few dead cats, rabbits and mice that had fallen into the well.

This created the need to shock the well water with a chlorine solution. After letting the chemical do its job for about 12 – 15 hours, the water was pumped out on to the front lawn.

This revealed the stone walls that went down about 15 - 20 feet. To keep the well from re-filling, we left the pump in place and would periodically turn it on when needed.

The Inspection

My dad lowered a ladder into the well to begin his investigation. He then climbed down into the well with a flashlight. My brother Bob held a flashlight as back up on the surface, and for additional light.

After the inspection, he began the clean and repair operation. This had to be done immediately after draining the well as it would immediately but slowly begin to refill requiring the drain pump.

The Repairs

Few repairs were needed as the well was soundly constructed. Most of the contamination came from the loose rotting wood cover that allowed the above-mentioned animals to enter.

We then placed several feet of washed clean gravel at the bottom of the well, to filter the new water coming in. We installed a new pipe from the well to the house.

We then poured a concrete cap all the way around the top of the well. The cap extended about 24 inches out from the edge of the well and slanted away from the opening.

In the cap, a 2-inch-wide ledge was created on four sides to a depth of 4-5 inches. A square concrete top would be inserted when done. It would rest on the ledge c/w handle for removal.

It was child-proof as it would take two adults at the ends of a crowbar to remove the concrete top. For further child proofing a large stone would be placed on top.

We then let the well refill, gave it another shock treatment washing the area above the water level and let it sit for 12 hours.

The well was once again pumped out to remove excess chlorine. We then let the well fill one last time, for our use.

Well water that is properly filtered in the well and capped at the top is usually as pure as it gets. We would do tests on a regular basis to make sure the water was contaminant free and fit to drink.

It always was after that.

The second well on the other side of the driveway underwent a similar change but we would rarely use it.

The Cistern in the Front Shed

The same cleaning process would take place in the cistern under the floor of the first shed. The floor opening, and access door were replaced and made structurally sound and rodent proof. Most importantly it was child-proof c/w lock.

This water was used for non-consumable household use such as cleaning and washing. It too would be tested for bacteria on a regular basis.

Drinking Water

A self-priming stainless-steel pump was placed in the basement of the house and connected to the pipe previously installed when the well was being repaired.

The pipe was below frost level and entered the well below the surface of the water travelling down to the lower part of the well. This was done during the earlier well maintenance and repair. It was ready before the final cleaning, chlorine treatment and water replacement.

The other end of the system went to a faucet in the kitchen that would direct the water into the sink. An electric on/off switch was installed to operate the pump.

To get water to drink or for cooking, you simply turned the switch on, and a stream of fresh clean water came out of the tap. The hand pump was no longer used and was removed.

Household Use

For household use in the kitchen and upstairs bathroom, my dad installed another pump that would supply a pressure tank in the basement and a hot water heater.

This supply came initially from the cistern in the font shed, next to the house. With the building of the pond and new well system, this would change.

Unfortunately, the bathtub would come much later in 1951. This meant the temporary use of a galvanized tub for our bathtub (normally used to provide drinking water for cows).

It was brought into the kitchen from the front shed, for the occasion. This would continue for another 8 to 10 months. Good job we did not get a lot of visitors at bath time. Occasionally friends of my parents would drop by and get a chuckle at the sight.

The Septic System

The existing septic system would not support five people. It was simply a leaching pit without any tile drainage system. No sooner had we finished the repair of the wells and cistern, and we were faced with putting in a proper septic tank and drainage system.

Having just arrived we had no contacts and did the job by hand using shovels. We erected a temporary outdoor facility and began our project. Luckily it was summer and not winter.

The system placement would be on the east lawn beside the house and take up almost the entire yard. We dug the large pit for the septic tank and had it delivered and installed. We then began digging the trenches for the drainage tiles.

We finished the trenches, placed a couple of inches of gravel in the bottom, and laid the tile. It was then time to start on the final backfilling of the trenches.

The area was levelled, and grass seed was planted. All the pipe connections were made, and the project was complete.

Finally, we were done, and everyone breathed a sigh of relief as we removed the outdoor facilities and filled in the hole.

Our Fall Projects 1950

In the fall of 1950 we would remove the screens from all the windows in the house and install the storm windows that had been stored in the basement. We would replace the screen door in the front shed with a storm door.

The Vegetable Garden - Fall 1950

In the fall of 1950 we would start preparation for the new garden. It would be much larger than the existing one. With the horse and plow we plowed a much larger section of land directly behind the house where the first garden had been.

INDOOR PROJECTS

Winter 1950/Early Spring 1951

The household renovations would be an ongoing *"work in progress"* project, and it would keep us occupied in the winter months and beyond.

One of the first projects was to remove some of the doors between the downstairs rooms.

The removal included kitchen/dining room, hallway/living room, one hallway door, and the double pane glass doors between the living room and dining room.

Replacing Wallpaper with Paint

During this period, we would remove the wall paper in every room downstairs and upstairs. This often meant removing 5 or 6 layers.

We would wet the top layer and use a flat scraper to remove the wallpaper layer by layer. If we were lucky two or more layers came off at once.

My mother oversaw the wallpaper removal and made sure that we did not slack off when on the job. She also took part and set the pace.

Room by room would see all the wall paper removed and a new coat of plaster applied over the old one. This was followed by sanding and a very good cleaning, before the paint could be applied.

My dad was in the paint business and was a perfectionist when it came to *"surface preparation"*. The perfectionism part would be even worse when applying the paint.

Under his supervision, we would all become experts at preparation, painting, edging and trim work.

The Floors Were Next

The kitchen floor was first. It was time to replace the ugly 10-foot-wide linoleum strips and all the patches. I remember the new flooring was 12-inch square tiles. They were not self-stick and had to be glued.

The two colours were grey and an orangey red (probably a hot 50's combination). The same removal and replacement would occur in the upstairs bathroom. Here they would use only the grey tiles.

Painted Wood Floors

It was then time to remove the grey paint on the floors in the rest of the house. This would involve many hours of sanding with a large sander.

Even with a collection bag, we would need to open windows (even on cold days).

This would be followed by hand sanding for areas the large sander could not reach. It would eventually be worth it.

Upstairs the sanding revealed the pine floors beneath. Downstairs the hardwood floors were exposed. We would stain and top coat with a clear varnish both upstairs and downstairs. The floor project took us almost four months to complete.

During the first years there would be many other house projects to keep all of us busy.

Modernization in the House

My mother took on the challenges of running a household of almost pioneer status with vigour and enthusiasm.

She would enjoy the changes that made her life easier. First came the new increased electrical amp system, along with some new wiring in the fall of 1950. These initial upgrades would make the other changes possible.

Christmas 1950

My mom got a new electrical cooking stove and oven. She would eagerly prepare our first Christmas dinner and put the leftovers in her other Christmas present, an electric powered refrigerator (no blocks of ice required).

My mom was now enjoying several of the conveniences and comforts, that she had left behind six months earlier. The wood stove remained to provide heat and would still be used for some baking and warming of coffee or hot chocolate.

I got my Lionel Electric train set that year. To this day, I still have the engine and all the cars. The tracks slowly disappeared over the years.

Christmas that year, would also equip us for our winter activities.

Outdoor Projects – Winters 50/51

During the first two winters, we would need to clear the driveway and areas around the barn by hand with shovels. It was a great family time as we would all take turns at the end of the shovels.

We would finish the activity with hot chocolate, that had been warming on the wood stove in the kitchen.

My dad would occasionally have his favourite Rye and ginger ale. This was only his treat, as we were all too young.

Because of those enjoyable family memories, I still enjoy shovelling snow and clearing the driveway today.

In 1951, the following year; our neighbour would often stop by with his bulldozer and clean everything. We were never upset as there always seemed to be enough snow to shovel.

MEMORIES OF 1951

Outdoor Projects - Early Spring 1951

The Large Drive Shed

In the early spring of 1951; with snow still on the ground, we would begin the dismantling of the large equipment barn opposite the house.

My dad felt it was structurally unsound and dangerous. It was also a bit of an eyesore. He had other plans for the area.

First came the removal of the corrugated roof, then the barn boards. This was done by hand and using the horses. It was mostly done by my dad and brother Bob.

My younger brother Brian and I did not escape the project as it became our job to remove the nails from the barn boards. Looking back, I should have kept the nails as they were the square type.

It was now time to dismantle the structure, and for this we would use the team of horses. A long large-diameter rope was attached to a support brace and one by one they were removed.

It was finally time to bring down the now very unstable columns and beams. It was a sight to see as the horses began the removal process. Finally, the tipping point came, and the entire structure came crashing to the ground.

During the entire process Brian and I would have to view everything from a safe distance. Safety was a major part of this and many other projects yet to come.

The horses then pulled the 14-inch square beams and posts to the yard beside the barn where they were neatly piled.

They would remain there untouched for many years. The garage would be left for several years.

The above picture shows our horse Trigger and our dog Laddie in the foreground. Behind them you can see the old garage still standing.

To the left of the garage lies the rubble of the old drive shed left after pulling the structure down with the horses Frank and Lauddie.

To the right of the garage is the manure spreader and wagon. In the far background is our neighbour's house.

The Garage was left

The Garden - Spring 1951

We would use the horses to disc and harrow the soil to make final preparation for planting.

We would go to the Palermo General Store to get our seeds. It seemed like we planted everything possible. There were peas, carrots, beans, beets, cucumbers, potatoes, squash, watermelons, pumpkins and even several rows of corn.

The planting and watching the sprouts come out of the ground was the fun part; but soon, came the need for weed control. This would become one of our daily chores to hoe a row.

It was fun to be able to go out and pick the vegetables for our meals. It would be the beginning of my mom's preserving from our very own garden.

The overgrown east lawn beside the house had strawberry plants, raspberries, wild grapes and even several plumb trees at the fence line.

The many other fence lines on the property, would provide pears, cherries, apples and more plumbs. This would provide the ingredients for homemade jams, pies and more preserves for the winter.

The Hired Help

Hiring extra help made sense for someone who was holding down a full-time job in Toronto.

It became necessity and a natural progression to reduce my dad's work load and enable him to modernize operations.

In preparation, we would enclose the open front porch to provide a room for our new hired help.

There was a door into the house already and we would add one to west side so that the new help could come and go without disturbing the family. Electric baseboard heaters were also added.

In 1951, the second year of living on the farm, we hired our first hired hand named Lloyd. He was a pack rack, but very wise in his ways. I remember that his view point was that everything had a potential future use.

This is possibly why I also am such a pack rat today.

He would pick up a piece of wood and say this is already made for something. He would store these items in a huge cabinet that he built from the barn boards that had been removed from the large implement shed.

Lloyd unfortunately had an addiction to betting on the horses and would disappear on his day off and would often return drunk, and usually broke.

I remember one time he returned with gifts for everyone as be had won big. It was sort of like Christmas as he handed out the gifts with a big grin on his face and delightful chuckle.

The day off eventually increased to 2 or 3 days and the drinking sometimes continued after returning. My dad took him to AA and tried to help him, as that was the way my dad was.

Eventually one-day Lloyd did not return from his day off, and he was sadly missed by all of us. My dad finally tracked him down and tried to help him. Lloyd moved on and disappeared completely and we never heard from him again.

The second hired hand was Peter. He was Dutch and would wear his wooden shoes all the time, even while doing his chores.

The third hired hand was Neil and he stayed the longest. One thing I remember about Neil was his huge appetite, which often meant him finishing up all the remaining food, before he left the table.

This also meant we all had to grab our share, before it disappeared.

The Old Gate and Pathway to the House

Brian, Laddie and me enjoying the first Spring

In late Spring of 1951, the dirt/mud path above was replaced by a concrete sidewalk and pad as shown below. It would save a lot of floor washing by my mother and washing of mud from our shoes and boots. I am sure it was one improvement we all enjoyed

Brian and Me
Sitting on our new concrete Pad

This would be our first full year without the previous owner Fred's help. We were on our own for the Spring Planting (seeding), haying, threshing and fall plowing.

A New Roof for the House

Somehow that summer, we would find enough time to put a new roof on the house replacing the green shingles with red ones.

The roof was badly in need of repair and was a project for all. My dad and the hired hand would do all the roof work, while my brother Bob would supply materials by way of a rope and steady the ladder when needed.

The Dump

The rest of us would gather the old shingles and put them in the back of the old Department of Highways truck, ready to go to the local dump.

Some local farmers had a dump at the back of their property that they had been using for many years. They were great places to explore. If I only had some of the *"junk"* now, that I used to find there.

My dad respected the environment and would not follow the examples set by some of our neighbours. The dump was a few miles away and was always an adventure to visit as well.

Painting the House

As soon as the roof was shingled, we began work on the painting of the house. The prep work to get ready for the paint, was a major task. Scraping the peeling paint, then wire brushing.

It seemed this part would never end.

My dad, Lloyd (hired hand) and my brother Bob did most of the painting in the upper part using ladders.

The rest of the crew; that was comprised of my mother, myself and Brian, would join the others in the painting of the lower area. Ladders were not required to do this part.

The Farm Projects 1951

There was never a lack of work, and the time before and after spring planting was allocated for repairing the fence lines on the farm.

Fencing

This repair and replacing of fence lines would become a continuing "work in process", and would continue well into the mid-50's.

In 1951, we would dig the post holes by hand with special augers and spoon shaped shovels for this process. Rocks were loosened with a large crow bar and removed with the round nose shovel.

It was a very slow going and would produce many blisters and very powerful arm muscles.

Fence repair was something that would be required anytime the cows were out grazing. They, like many humans, felt that the pasture on the other side of the fence, was greener and would probably taste better.

Often, we would come home from school to find both our mother and father mending or working on the fences.

It often found the whole family digging holes, installing posts and stringing the fences.

My dad was a perfectionist when it came to installation of the posts. The posts had to be perfectly perpendicular in all directions. (without exception).

We would spend many hours helping to repair and install the fences. This too became great family time; and although hard work, was very enjoyable and satisfying.

Fall of 1951

The Chicken Project

During the winter of 1951/1952, we would expand the area for our chickens by renovating four horse stalls in the north/west corner of the west side. We would increase our laying hens from 12 to over 300.

One of the neighbouring farms (The Popes) was a chicken farm. It had a large barn with three floors of laying hens.

The Beginning

We started with chicks supplied by Mr. Pope, and used the remaining horse stalls to keep them contained. We would keep them warm using incubators borrowed and later purchased, from Mr. Pope.

We would later use the incubators to hatch our own chicks.

New nests were built, and it would soon become part of our chores (Brian and I) to feed the chickens and collect the eggs from the increased chicken population.

The Nests

My mom would wash and grade the eggs and put them in cartons for my dad. We would always save the double yokes for our breakfasts.

My dad would supply many of his paint customers with eggs as well as the Palermo General Store.

The Washing and Grading

He soon developed a large customer base and I often wondered why his boss did not complain. Maybe it was all the free eggs and chicken dinners that he enjoyed.

Having so many chickens meant a lot of chicken dinners for us as well. We did not go the local store and get our chickens that were ready to cook.

One of us would hold the chicken's feet while our mother chopped off their head. She would pluck all the feathers by hand and remove the final bits of the feather still in the chicken with tweezers.

After this she had to remove the innards and then clean the inside of the chicken in a brine solution. The outside of the chicken was also washed in a brine solution and dried.

It was now ready to cook or wrap and store in our new freezer, until needed. The freezer was in the basement.

We would also raise cattle for our own food, but fortunately for us, we would have the butcher in Milton, Ontario take care of the process. We would store the beef in the large freezer along with the chickens.

A freezer also meant ice cream. Often it was not store bought. My mom would make it from scratch.

My dad getting the last taste of ice cream

The Bakery Delivery

Our bread was delivered, and we would look forward to the weekly visits as it often meant a large bag of goodies. The bags were day-olds, and about 3 feet high by 20- 30 inches in diameter.

They were always full of deserts that we bought for next to nothing. In them would be donuts (many jelly filled) pies, tarts, cakes and lots of rolls and bread. It was one of our favourite events.

The bag of day old deserts and bread did not stop my mom from baking her own bread or making tarts and pies. They were always far better than what we found in the bag, but the bag was an adventure.

My mom would also get regular visits from the Watkins man and there were always lots of interesting items to see for house and barn use. After his visit, it was almost like Christmas.

Christmas 1951

Now age seven, I would experience a tradition that has also all but disappeared with emails and computes. My mother would purchase Christmas cards and send them to all our relatives and friends.

It would start with the purchase of the Christmas cards which was usually done through someone in our church.

Our mom would address them in long hand and include a message on the inside of the card. Her long hand was about as perfect as it gets, and I would not ever witness anything better.

By 1951 she had several hundred cards to address and send. The numbers would continue to grow through the years.

It would take a few weeks to finish them and Brian and I would put on the stamps and Christmas seals. The kitchen table was where most of this activity took place.

This was great fun, but the most exciting part was getting our cards in the mail each day and getting the news from everyone. Our house would be decorated with hundreds of cards on the walls everywhere.

It was the perfect build to Christmas day and presents under the tree.

For Christmas 1951 the family would get a black and white TV. We were the first ones in the neighbourhood to get one. Even with the large tower on the east side of the house we maybe got 2 channels, and on rare occasions we got 3.

All the kids in the neighbourhood would flock to our house after school and on weekends to watch. After school would never be the same.

What we Watched

For us there was Roy Rogers, Wild Bill Hickock, the Lone Ranger, and Howdy Doody.

Christmas that year, would also re-equip us for our winter activities with the next size up in skates, and sleighs.

Skating in 1951/2

The valleys in the front and middle east fields provided our natural skating rinks once again that year. They stretched from several fields back right to the road at the front of our property.

It seemed like we could skate forever. The areas were only around 12 inches deep and offered safe skating. There were many days skating, but it would be the moonlit nights skating through the fields, hearing only the skates, that I remember the most.

Tobogganing

Day or night, we would head out the fields to try our new toboggans and sleighs. We had many hills on the farm for tobogganing and sleighing.

After tying them all, we decided that the best hills were directly behind the barn by the hydro towers. In later years, we would add skiing to our list of activities.

The fence lines would often create huge drifts where we would make our forts.

**View from the West Lawn in December
Looking South West**

**View from the end of the Driveway
Looking North/West at our bush**

The previous picture shows the second gateway to the equipment staging area. House and barn are on the right just out of the picture. The entrance to the lane, fields and the bush is to the left.

The view above is from the start of the lane
Looking North/West

In the foreground it shows the entrance to the laneway that goes to the back of the property and the bush. In the background we see the west side of our bush at the back of the farm.

MEMORIES OF 1952

The Sad Changes

Although very romantic; and part of my fondest memories of the farm, the old ways would sadly begin to change. This was to make life easier; or in our case, to allow us to increase the workload capabilities.

In the early summer of 1952, we would get our first tractor along with some attachments to re-place several pieces of horse drawn equipment. These attachments would significantly reduce the field work, time and effort required.

It was the smaller Allis Chalmers model, and it came with a font end loader, a mower attachment for cutting hay and post hole digger to replace the digging of post holes by hand.

The front-end loader was used for many jobs, including loading the manure into the spreader and clearing the barnyard area of snow in the winter.

The front driveway snow removal was still on the family to do manually list. On bad snow days, our neighbour Dave Wendover would drop by with his bulldozed and plow everything.

Often when he was done, Dave and my dad would sit in our kitchen and have a few rye and gingers. (protection against the cold they would say)

The Mechanical Age Begins

In the summer of 1952, we would begin using the small tractor to cut the hay and later to rake it ready for final curing and collection.

Memories of our Horses

This summer would be the last year that we would use the horses to bring the hay into the barn. There would be no experience that could replace the comradeship of man and horses working together.

The horses knew their duties and often when the hay wagon was full and the hayloader was unhitched, they would not need any directions or commands.

On their own, they would begin the trip back to the barn. We would just lie back, close our eyes, enjoy the fragrance of the hay and the motion of the swaying wagonload.

Often, we would chew the sweet end of a timothy stalk. (a type of hay) It was the cool farmer thing to do.

When we arrived back at the barn, the horses would stop and eagerly await the next part of their duties. It was strange how the horses enjoyed the challenges and work each day.

After work, they would happily munch on a reward of grain. They would then join the cows, after the evening milking was done, and they all travelled back to the field set aside for pasture.

The next morning, they would join the cows on their way back to the barn, ready for the beginning of another day.

The horses were very gentle and had a great sense of humour that they sometimes displayed.

They would get excited at the appearance of the harnesses and occasionally run and kick both back feet in the air, in anticipation of the day ahead.

Sometimes they would pick up part of a harness in their teeth and bring it too one of us, as if to say: "Let's get this show on the road".

More Changes

In the fall of 1952, we would get a larger Allis Chalmers tractor to take care of the heavier tasks such as plowing the fields with our new three-furrow-plow.

With its power take off wheel we could also now do our own threshing and wood cutting using the belt and pully system.

In the fall of 1952, we would purchase our own threshing machine. We were now totally independent and no longer had to wait in line to do our threshing.

It sadly meant the disappearance of the community and social nature of threshing that we had once enjoyed, especially the very large dinners on the west lawn.

Home Improvements

We started removing the old wire and post fences around the house to get ready for the ranch style fences that would soon replace them on the east, west and south sides.

Driveway Entrance

The two pictures above show the south front fence has already been removed in preparation for the new one. The west fence is still there and will be removed next.

The New Fence looking north from road

The new ranch style fence stretched across the front. The old wire fence next to the driveway on the west side of the house is gone. We would not replace, it as it was better without one.

View from neighbour's farm
Looking North/West

Front fence is painted. - East fence is on the to do list.

Recreational Projects in 1952

At the House

The west side of the driveway where the old equipment shed had been, was set aside for recreational use. We planted grass and built a white brick BBQ.

On the southern most part, we groomed the soil to put in a putting green c/w flags. It was the area closest to the road. We would also replace the old wire fencing across the front of the property on the west side of the driveway, with a white ranch-style fence.

Christmas 1952

Brian and I would once again get re-outfitted with our winter sports equipment.

Looks like Laddie wants some skis as well

Laddie once again asking for skis

Christmas will also include more western outfits for the summer of 1953. We had been watching the western TV shows all summer in 1952, including the new series of Hopalong Cassidy.

It was perfect timing to get my complete Hoppy outfit with black hat, black shirt, western tie, holsters and guns.

Above I am wearing one of my western outfits that I found under the Christmas tree.

**Here I am again western style
c/w hat, shirt, chaps and guns**

Above I am on Pepper. It was one of the horses being boarded that we could ride. This picture is on the west lawn looking south.

MEMORIES OF 1953

Beyond the Hired Help Days

After the hired help years of 1951 and 1952, it became part of the duties of the three sons to help manage the growing work load on the farm.

On a farm, one learned how to drive horses, operate equipment and milk cows, at an early age. Now at 15, my brother bob helped my dad with most duties including milking and the field work.

I was only six when we arrived and was assigned the very simple tasks such as collecting eggs, getting the cows and collecting vegetables from the small garden and wild fruit from the many locations on the farm.

In 1953 after the end of the hired help, both my younger brother Brian now 6 and myself now 9 would take on many more responsibilities. We shared putting down straw for bedding, and hay when required to feed the cows and horses.

Fencing Repair and Replacement

The posthole digger attachment, added a whole new dimension to fencing. It was now done on a much larger scale than before. This meant we could now speed up the fencing process significantly.

We now brought the cedar posts in by the truckload. This created another chore for my younger brother Brian and myself. It was peeling the bark off the posts for the fences, for better weathering.

We would spend many hours during the summer with our jack-knives, peeling the bark off logs at 25 cents for each log completed.

New fencing would now become an ongoing front burner project to replace the old fences. It would remain a priority, until all the old fences were replaced.

After replacing them all, it became an ongoing repair and maintenance operation.

Adding more Land for Farming

With the introduction of the tractors the workload in the summer would lessen, but only for a short time. With all this new equipment making our work so much easier, we would begin to add more farmland.

In the fall of 1953, we would rent the first available land which would be on our neighbour's 100-acre farm (Dave Wendover) which was immediately on our west side.

In the fall, we would start plowing several fields on this property, with our new tractor driven three-furrowed-plow.

Keeping Some Traditions

This year, we would continue to use the horses and binder to cut the grain and put it into sheaves and would begin to do our own threshing using our own threshing machine.

We would continue to have lunches on the west lawn this year and for many future years, in the summer during haying and threshing seasons.

Visitors to the Farm

Each year would see more relatives visiting the farm in the summer. I think we were now the place to go for an outing on the weekends. Russell would return for his annual farming 101 lessons.

This year would see a new comer as my mom's sister would bring her adopted daughter for a weeklong visit for the first time.

Here I am on the left while my cousin takes the wheel. Brian is crunched over to the right of her. Behind us is the old garage still standing.

The New Pond

In the spring of 1953, it was time to contract our neighbour Dave Wendover (local contracting and excavation) to install our new pond.

Just west of the house in the front west field, we would create a huge pond to provide household water, barn water and recreational swimming and skating.

The pond level would be low in its creation, as it had not yet had a spring run-off to fill its banks. This would happen in the Spring of 1954.

Below the Pond Under Construction

Looking north/west, we see the tree line border of our farm in the distance and Dave's barn on the other side.

Shaping the Pond

Above we are looking at the south west corner of our farm with the large elm trees on the west and south sides.

Below my dad (in his paint hat) watching the progress

We are now looking north/east, with our barn very close as a backdrop for all the excavation activity.

The New Well

Beside the pond, about 10 feet away at the deep south end, we would install a concrete tile well about four feet in diameter by 20 feet deep.

It was set on clean gravel with several feet in the well itself for final filtration of the well water.

A trench was made from the pond to the bottom of the well. It too was filled with clean gravel. The gravel would filter the water from the pond before it entered the well.

The well was gravity fed as the pond was higher than the bottom of the well. The well top would be about 30 inches above ground level.

Above we see our whole family standing in the deep end of the empty pond. The pond is now finished, and water is starting to fill it.

Only about 12 feet higher to go. The pond was starting to fill as we see on the left side of the picture. By the end of the year, where we are standing the water would be about five feet high.

Below, we have finished digging the trench and are installing the concrete sections for the well.

Above: My dad and Laddie Supervising

The third tile is almost in place with two more tiles to go plus the top, and the well is in place. We will finish adding the clean gravel and then backfill the ditch with the soil from the dig.

Supply to House 1953

A trench was then made below frost level from the pond to the house. In it we would place a 2-inch diameter black polyvinyl flexible pipe. It would connect the pond well to the pump in the house.

The pond well was now connected to the pump and pressure tank in the house. We would now discontinue the daily use of the cistern for household water. The water from the eves trough, was now directed to the lawn area.

Cleaning of Existing Ponds

We had two other ponds already existing on the farm that supplied water for the cows and horses when they were out in the pasture areas.

They had become almost mud swamps over the years of constant use in the pasturing months. They needed refurbishing.

When finishing the font field pond, it made sense to make the necessary improvements while the excavating equipment was there on our property.

The first pond to be repaired was the one in the lane that protruded into the east middle field. With the same large shovel as we used for the well, the mud was scooped out of the expired pond and placed to one side next to the lane to be later removed.

The second pond at the bush was next to undergo a similar refurbishing.

The two ponds would take several days to remove the mud and create fresh new ponds. It was the intent to dump the mud removed into a low area in one of the other fields.

Tragedy Beckoned

It was during the second evening that our horse Trigger would become trapped in the mud from the lane pond. When we went to get the cows in the morning, we would find our horse in the mud with only his head and neck visible.

Totally exhausted from his efforts to free himself, it appeared that he was not going to survive his ordeal. The mud had made breathing a difficult process and he was panting and gasping for air.

The bulldozer arrived and began to remove the mud around trigger while others used hand shovels and their bare hands to clear away the mud.

When most of the mud was cleared away from his legs ropes were tied around all four legs and the bull dozer slowly pulled him out of the mud.

The rescue effort had taken over three hours, and his survival was questionable. He was too weak to stand so we knelt beside him and used pails of water and towels to wash the remaining mud away.

The local vet Doc Heslop had arrived and provided some shots of something to assist his recovery.

During this time, we kept talking to him and stroking his nose to show we were there. After what seemed like an eternity he showed signs of wanting to stand.

All work on the bush pond had come to a halt as everyone had become involved in the rescue effort. There was no shortage of manpower to help him to his feet.

There were about six or seven people holding him while he found his legs and could stand on his own. There were cheers of joy as it now seemed that Trigger would survive his ordeal.

Earlier we had brought hay, water and grain out to the location in anticipation of the success of our efforts. We now stayed with him until he found the strength to walk.

The crews would return to their work at hand and that day all the excavated mud was spread on the designated fields and would no longer be a safety threat to animals or humans.

It would take 3 or 4 days for Trigger to become his old self. During the next two days, everyone involved in the rescue would pay several visits to check up on their patient.

Unfortunately, Trigger was now afraid of mud and would stop short of any mud puddle large or small while riding him. It took some time to get over this fear.

Recreational Development

While my dad was at his sales job Bob, Brian and I would work on the recreational areas by the house when not doing our other chores.

We had now added horseshoe pits in the area on the west side of the driveway along with adding the finishing touches on the putting green.

We also started work on an area to play badminton in the small field between the house and new pond.

By mid-summer, we began to groom the area around the pond and planted grass. By next summer we would be cutting it.

It became our job to cut the grass around the house, the entire recreational area west of the driveway plus the soon to be added, area around the pond.

RECREATIONAL LAYOUT PLANS IN 1953

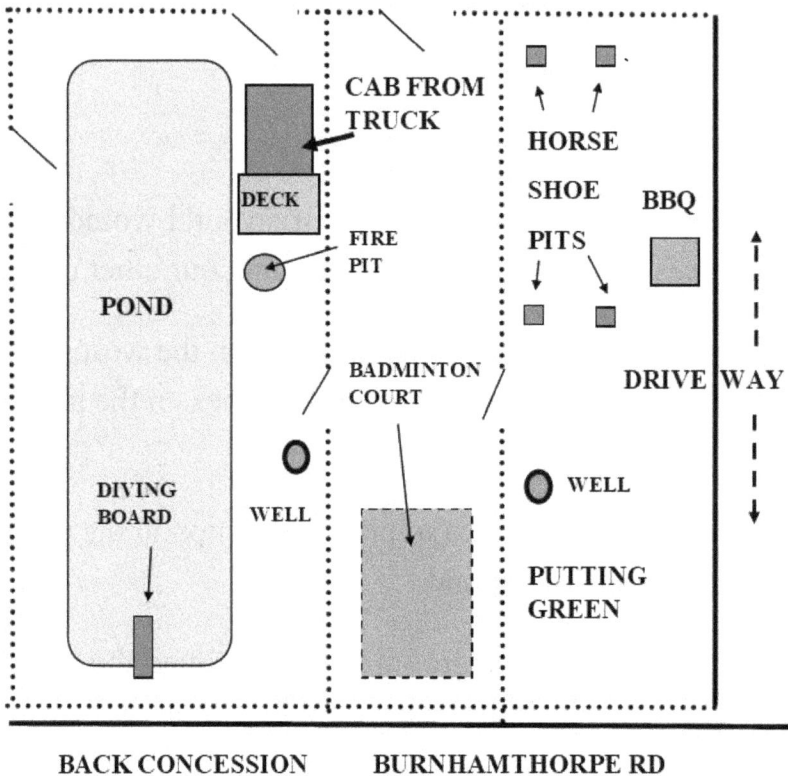

BACK CONCESSION   BURNHAMTHORPE RD

Pond Activities

During the first two summers after its creation, we would have the use of the pond for swimming pretty much to ourselves.

The first newcomers to the pond (the frogs) appeared in the fall of 1953 in the first year. They would add their voices at night to the ever-present sound of crickets in the fields.

The frogs would often appear on the surface with their noses just above the water, to obtain air. They did not interrupt our swimming activities.

Late Summer Swimming the First year
Water levels are still low

The Pond in the Fall

The first fall 1953 would bring the wild ducks to stop over on their trip south. This became an annual event. They would also include a stopover in the spring on their return.

Often, they would hatch their young and we would watch their young grow to the point of flying, before they would all travel further north.

The Pond in the Winter

In 1953 our winter activities added skating and hockey on the new pond with our new skates and hockey sticks and official pucks.

It was a good size after the summer and fall rains. The pond became a winter playground. Once the ice was thick enough, we would begin clearing the snow.

There would be many moonlit nights spent shovelling the pond surface.

Year One Winter Activities

With Pond still at a Low Level

Our neighbours across the road would also help in the clearing as they too enjoyed the skating activity.

The sound of the skates and the wood shovel; that we built for the occasion, is something I will never forget. At night, there would be a special extra ring to this activity.

I would have a huge crush on the girl (Janice) across the road. She was my older brothers age. That did not stop me from requesting the hand holding skates around the pond with her.

There would be many hockey games played and many days and nights of just plain skating. We would build our own goals using wood from the old drive sheds and chicken wire left over from the chicken coup.

Often after a snowfall we would first create a series of paths and a maze in the snow. It was great fun to race to the finish line. After creating new paths and blocking old ones, the adventure continued.

We would sit on the benches made from the lumber of the old drive shed. There would be many night time fires when there was no moon to light the way for our skating activities, and yes, even more attempts at hand holding.

The fires also provided a source to cook winter hot dogs and roast marshmallows. On a few daring nights when it was not very cold, we would sleep in the cab of the truck that we had removed from the Department of Highways truck.

We would take turns feeding the fire to keep warm. This usually meant several check-ups during the night by our parents, to make sure we all were OK.

Christmas 1953

Christmas 1953 I remember because I would get my very own 200 shot automatic Daisy Red Ryder BB gun.

Here I am probably aiming at tree

The movie **"*A Christmas Story*"** produced in 1983 about a boy wanting a BB gun for Christmas brings back fond memories of that Christmas.

MEMORIES OF 1954

After the Spring Run-off 1954

The pond would now reach adulthood with new dimensions of about 70+ feet across by 350+ feet long and around 12-15 feet deep at the south end. It tapered off to inches where the water entered on the north end.

At the south end closest to the road, in the south/west corner was the spillway. This controlled the size of the pond and kept the water fresh.

The Pond

During the summer of 1954, we would build a farm fence on all four sides of the pond using our new post hole digger.

We would further renovate the cab from the old department of highways truck that we had purchased. We had placed it at the north/east end by the pond, the year before (1953).

The cab would be used for storage, and after adding curtains, we would also use it as a change area. The fold down seats were great to sit on and watch the fires that we would have.

Behind the seats were shelves where we would keep kindling, paper and matches for starting our fires. There was also room for a good supply of wood.

We soon extended the floor inside the cab and added a large platform in front of the cab for out tent and lawn chairs. We would spend many nights sleeping at the pond listening to the birds, crickets and frogs and watching the stars.

We placed a diving board at the deep end (about 12 – 15 feet deep) and would also have many contests for the best dive or cannon ball.

Looking South/East

Looking South

The pond would become the local swimming spot for us, for our neighbours, friends and our many visitors. We can see people waiting to use the diving board at the deep end.

The Log Game

We would use posts previously designated for our fences. We would sit on one end in the water and the other end would stick out of the water on a 45-degree angle.

We would ride them, steering and moving about using our hands and legs as paddles. One game that we used to play was to knock our opponents off their log.

The Log Survival Game

A Participant – Looks like Brian

It was great fun and often there would be teams with two or more on each side. As each person was knocked off they would no longer take part until winners or a winner was created.

We also tied four or five logs together for a raft. We would take a sleeping bag and place it on the raft and drift about the pond.

Nature Moves In

The summer of 1954, would bring some bull-rushes and many birds as new inhabitants. Two of my favourite birds were the red-winged blackbird and the killdeer.

Their distinctive calls would become an enjoyable start and end to many days. Swallows would build their nests in the bulrushes and the whole area was now alive.

The blue herons had come this summer and now walked the shallows searching for food.

In this, the second year, the pond would see an increased growth of weeds and bulrushes around the entrance of the pond as seeds had been carried into the pond with the spring run-off.

The pond remained the hub of activities with much swimming, bonfires and camping out.

The rest of the recreational areas would add to the enjoyment of the non-working times. It was decided that in the spring of 1955, we would add fish to the pond so that we could enjoy recreational fishing.

Our People Visitors

We had many visitors (mostly relatives from the city). The pond would become the place to go to when company arrived.

My cousins from Stratford, Ontario would become frequent visitors. Jack Salter was Bobs age and Russel Hause was my age. Every year Russel would come for two or three weeks in the summer. In return I would go to his house in Stratford.

My father's boss would spend many weekends camped at the pond and enjoying the country life. He would stretch out on his lawn chair, read a book and get a tan.

He also loved riding the logs and even took part in a couple of contests.

My uncle Jim Shillum was another frequent guest who would spend time swimming and tanning himself by the pond.

Trigger

Everyone who visited the farm wanted to ride our horse Trigger. They would have their picture taken on the horse as a memento of their visit.

The Farming Activities Continued

In 1954, we would harvest the existing hay crops on the newly acquired 100 Acres obtained in the fall of 1953. We had already plowed several fields with our new tractor driven three-furrowed-plow.

In 1954 Bob was now 16, Brian was 7 and I was 10. This year I would add raking hay with the small tractor, to my summer duties.

After first driving the horses and then driving the tractor to collect the loose hay, it was a natural progression and my introduction to the heavier field work.

In the beginning, the raking by me was only in short intervals on very flat land. My father would always be working close by to keep an eye on my apprentice activity.

My father was very big on safety and taught us all very well. Many people today might be alarmed at driving a tractor and equipment at age 10, but it was not unusual for a farm boy in those days.

In 1954, we would see the end of bringing in loose hay using the tractor, as we now introduced baled hay.

At first, we subcontracted the baling, but lack of control would soon cause us to purchase our own baler.

Baling the Hay

With the new hay and straw packaging in bales, came a new challenge. It would be building loads that would not fall off. We would also make this a family competition to see who could build the best loads.

A partially built load

There would be many hills on the way home from our other farms. Many loads would fall backwards, sideways and frontwards. It was always a challenge to get home and up the ramp without a spill.

More Land

In the fall of 1954, we would rent a second 100-acre farm just west of us, on the south/west corner of the town line and our road. (The Fax Ball property).

We would plow fields to be ready for planting of oats in the spring.

Painting the Barn

The painting of the barn was started in 1952 but my dad did not like green and ended it with half the front painted.

This time the painting of the barn would become an ongoing project starting in the late spring. It continued all summer and ended early fall of 1954.

For my dad, painting was not just a matter of applying paint to the roof and barn boards. It was a carefully planned professional process.

To this day I do not know how he found the courage, energy or the time to complete the farming and handle these enormous tasks, while successfully holding down his sales job.

Cleaning and Painting the Roof

It would be necessary (by my dad's rules) to remove *"ALL"* of the old peeling paint first, with an electric powered wire brush, then hand scrape and finally wire brush. Each day the part just cleaned would need to be prime painted as well.

The roof cleaning and painting was a long process and would take many days and part days, to complete the task. The process would see the roof cleaned and prime painted in stages. Once the Cleaning and priming on the first side was done, the final top coat was applied using the same handling and safety process.

Access and Safety

Rule One: Only my dad could do the cleaning and painting of the roof.

Rule # Two: What was cleaned had to be primed on the same day as it was cleaned.

How he did the Cleaning

On one side of the barn opposite the side where the work was taking place, would be the tractor. A long 1-inch diameter rope was attached to it.

The rope was thrown over the peak of the barn roof and down the other side. The rope had many loops to hang onto, and it also had a safety harness attached to it, in case my dad let go of the rope.

A ladder reaching past the eves trough was then tied to the barn on the side where the work was taking place.

The Equipment for Cleaning the Roof

The equipment for cleaning was an electric powered wire brush. It was tied to a small rope that was also thrown over the roof from the other side. This was done to lessen the weight of the long electric cord.

The hand scraper and hand-held wire brush were tied around his waist and were ready for use when needed.

Painting the Roof

After cleaning a strip of about 15 to 20 feet wide, it was then primed with a red oxide primer.

To do a full strip, was an all-day job to complete both the cleaning and painting. If less time was available, it usually meant a smaller portion of roof would be cleaned and then prime painted.

When a full strip (top to bottom) was done, the tractor was moved and the next 15 to 20-foot strip would be cleaned and prime painted. This continued until the first side of the roof was cleaned and prime painted.

The Painting Process

This meant holding on to the rope with one hand and spray painting with the other.

A small rope attached to the tractor, was also thrown over the roof to the other side that was being painted. It was attached about 10 feet from the end where the spray gun was, to lessen the weight.

The position of the small rope would be changed to suit the area being painted. As my dad moved down the roof toward the bottom and eves trough, the small rope, hoses and spray gun would be extended.

This provided the freedom to move about and paint a large area.

The Equipment

Located on the side being painted, we would use a very large pressure pot to hold the paint supply.

A very large compressor (my uncle Jim's) would provide the air required for the pot and spray guns. Two long hoses were connected from the supply end (pressure pot) to the other end where the spray gun was located.

One hose supplied the paint and the other supplied the air to control the spray gun. They would be carried up the ladder and onto the roof by my dad.

The small rope connected to the hoses would be pulled from the other side and take up the slack until my dad was in position to start painting.

The compressor and pressure tank were placed on our truck on the side that was being painted, so they could easily be moved to where the painting was taking place.

Above my dad at the peak of the roof

The Dept. of Highways truck at ground level holding the Compressor and paint pot.

Note: our cat in the bottom left corner, I am just behind it and to the right behind me on the other side of the fence is Brian.

A closer look at my dad

Top Coat on Roof

Before moving to the other side of the barn, the second or top coat of the colour white was applied. This was quicker because no cleaning was needed.

After completing the top coat on side one, both the tractor and truck reversed positions with each moving to the opposite side of the barn.

Side Two

The same procedure would take place all over again until the second side of the roof was cleaned, primed and top coated. Two additional people would always be present to steady the ladder even though it was tied to the barn. One person was usually my mother and I would be the other.

One of us would also look after adjusting the small rope attached to the spray gun. Brian who was now 7 would be a back up. Often, Brian and I would hold the ladder while my mom took a well-deserved breather.

Stepping over the Edge

The view is from the bottom as seen by the person designated to steady the ladder. It's a long way up or down depending on your view point.

After what seemed like an eternity to all of us (the helpless spectators), both sides of the roof were completed.

Painting the Barn

The next part would be the painting of the four sides of the barn. Once again, the compressor and pressure tanks were placed on our truck, to follow the painting process.

Travelling up almost 60 feet at the peaks on the ends of the barn to first clean and then paint was not an easy task.

It made painting the lower part on the ends and the front and back of the barn walls, seem easy by comparison. Here the painter (my dad) would only reach a height of about 35 to 40 feet.

It would take the rest of spring, all summer and into the fall of 1954 to complete this task. We would paint the barn white this time.

A second coat was needed to hide the green portion started previously. Two years later my dad would paint the entire barn white again to provide a full hiding coat on the roof and sides.

The attention given by my dad's cleaning and painting efforts has resulted in a paint job that is still there. It is faded somewhat, but still in reasonably good shape for its age some 61 years later.

The Surge Milking Parlour 1954

With all this new activity created by modernization, you might think there was little else to modernize. This thought would have been wrong.

In the summer of 1954 we would now begin work on a new milking parlour. It would be located on the west side of the barn (Area 3).

It would mean the removal of the remaining horse stalls and eventual re-location of the recently created chicken coop facilities in stages.

The chickens would make the final move to Area One (the old milking location) when the milking parlour became operational.

There would be extensive renovations including creation of two levels in the new milking parlour and a new milk room for the milk storage tank.

In 1954 a new water supply line would be installed to the barn from the house for the new milking facilities. A hot water tank was added along with an oil-fired stove to heat the area.

October 1954 Hurricane Hazel

Everything would be interrupted on our farm, with the almost unexpected arrival of Hurricane Hazel.

To top it off, we had had very high amounts of rain just prior to the storms arrival and the ground was saturated.

This would mean almost no ground absorption capabilities and the water now traveled at high speeds and created a high amount of soil erosion.

Hazel was logged as an extra tropical Category 1 storm.

With winds of 68 miles per hour (110 Kilometers) also came the rainfall of over 11 inches (285 millimeters) in 48 hours. The storm would last for three days. (*info from Wikipedia)*

Our pond soon disappeared, the small field with the badminton court was under water.

The water flooded the driveway and reached half way up the west lawn of the house. The barnyard was under water as well as the lower end of the laneway.

The front east field normally had an intermittent stream running through the wide valley. Here, the water reached part way up the hill next to the house, on the east side.

The road was under water to a depth of several feet.

The front west field had a deeper valley and would reach a depth of 10 to 12 feet and totally flood the road to a depth of 4 or 5 feet. All the way back to the bush the low-lying fields on both sides were under water.

The storm left such devastation everywhere, that the name Hazel would never be used again for an Atlantic hurricane.

What Hazel Did to the Farm

As the water levels dropped we began to see the damage left behind. Around the pond much of the new grass had been swept away and large craters had been created on all sides of the pond.

A huge amount of debris and soil from the fields and fence lines had found its way into the pond. Where the run-off had been to control the level of the pond, there was a very deep crater in the ground.

Next to the house the putting green was no more. The horseshoe pits were destroyed, the basement of the house had filled to a level of about six inches. Sump pumps averted any major damage here.

In the barn, the old milking area was temporarily under water and would need to be totally cleaned. In the fields, there were now many crevasses on the hills that now needed to be filled in to make the fields farmable.

The end of 1954 and early 1955 would become a major clean-up operation, and the beginning of a slow recovery from the storm.

Christmas 1954

One of the other Christmases that would also stand out in my memory, was the year I would get my single shot Ranger 22 rifle. I would also get my official Davey Crocket racoon hat.

Trapping

After watching the Walt Disney series Davey Crocket, I decided to embark on my new career. With my trusty rifle and official coonskin hat, I was ready to start trapping. I took some old traps I had found in the barn and set out to make my fortune selling the furs.

I would attend my trap line in the bush every day. After several weeks of this and no luck, I would buy some snare wire. I added this with hopes of changing my luck.

At the end of about four or five weeks without any results, I decided that I would not make my fortune here. The outings had been enjoyable and had brought me closer to nature, so not all was lost.

I collected all my traps and snare wire and bid farewell my trapping career.

MEMORIES OF 1955

The Surge Milking Parlor 1955

In 1955, we would see the end of the old milking facilities and a change to modern day milking as shown below. It would be totally automated as milk now went right from the cow to the milk cooler.

A 2-inch clear glass pipe would connect the milking machine directly into the cooler. Because of the vacuum created in it by its own compressor, it would pull the milk down the pipe and into the cooler.

With this automated and much easier method of milking came an increase to 30 milking cows.

LAYOUT OF NEW MILKING PARLOR

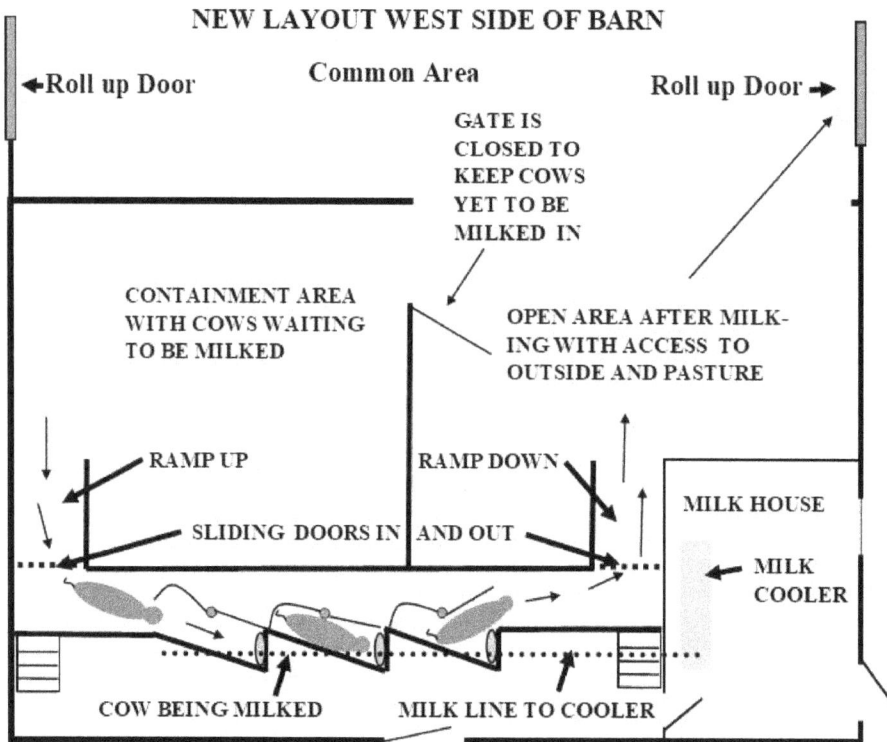

NEW LAYOUT WEST SIDE OF BARN

◄Roll up Door   Common Area   Roll up Door ➡

GATE IS CLOSED TO KEEP COWS YET TO BE MILKED IN

CONTAINMENT AREA WITH COWS WAITING TO BE MILKED

OPEN AREA AFTER MILK-ING WITH ACCESS TO OUTSIDE AND PASTURE

RAMP UP   RAMP DOWN

MILK HOUSE

SLIDING DOORS IN AND OUT

MILK COOLER

COW BEING MILKED   MILK LINE TO COOLER

How it Worked

A ramp up was created to allow the cow to enter the milking parlour. The person milking would pull open a sliding door to allow the next cow to be milked into the parlour.

There were three stalls and each stall had a chute from the second floor grainery into a small feeding box. As an incentive, each cow was given a mixture of oats and meal when they entered the stall by flipping a lever.

The area below the raised part for the cows, had been further excavated to allow the person milking, to easily wash the cow and attach the milking machine while in a standing position.

The raised area for the cows had a 2-inch concrete curb and a tubular barrier to prevent the cow from going over the edge. There were concrete stairs at either end with a gate, to allow access to the raised area.

There were three sets of gates that opened at one end to let the cow into one of the three stalls. When the milking was finished the gate at the other end of the stall would be opened, and the cow was let out.

Three Cows Being Milked

191

The New Milk Cooler

After being milked and let out of the stall, the exit door was pulled open. In the summer, the cow could continue to the pasture.

In the winter, they could roam the closed in barnyard or stay in the barn open area where they were fed hay.

Equipment Cleaning

Unlike the old method of hand washing the milking equipment, it was now completely automated. Once the milking was done, the three sets of milking machines were taken to the room with the cooler.

The three milking machine attachments were given an initial rinse in a separate tank and then placed into the tank of the automatic cleaning system.

It was an open stainless-steel tank approximately 24 inches wide x 48 inches long x 30 inches deep, where the milking machines were placed. The machines were then connected to the cleaning system.

The glass pipe that carried the milk to the cooler from the parlour was unfastened from the cooler and connected to the cleaning system.

The time for the cleaning was set and the tank of the cleaning system would fill with a safe germ cleaning solution. When the small tank was full, a float switch would signal a vacuum pump at the far end of the system.

The vacuum pump would then suck the solution from the small tank through the milking machine attachments, through the length of glass pipe, and store it in its large reservoir.

When full, the reservoir would now act as a pressure pump and flush the solution back through the glass pipe and through the milking machines and into its original tank.

After repeating the cleaning cycle several times, it would drain and then undergo several rinse cycles and finally drain and shut off. When it was time for the next milking, the glass pipe was re-connected to the cooler and we were ready to start milking.

Community Work 1955

The painting of the barn the previous year had caused quite a stir in the community. The minister of our church approached my dad to paint the church and parish hall white.

Of course, being the person that he was, my dad agreed to take on the task. A request for help was announced during several sermons, and the date was set to begin the task.

Once again, my father's surface preparation requirements would have to be met. Most of the volunteers felt that the preparation part was unnecessary, and fewer and fewer would show up to do this part.

My older Brother Bob was now 17 and I was 11 and Brian was 8. Along with several remaining volunteers, we would make up most of the surface preparation and pre-treatment crew and finish the scraping, wire brushing and sanding.

The main painting was pretty much done by my father, while the rest of us would take turns holding the ladder and looking after the trim work. When the church was done, it was time to do the parish hall.

Farm Repair and Maintenance

1955 had begun with much excavation and use of our front-end loader. Many large craters and holes left by the storm would need to be filled in. It would take many weeks in the spring to repair the damage.

The End of an Era

In the fall of 1955, we would stop using the binder to make sheaves. This would in turn, end the stooking and threshing. These operations would now be achieved by using a combine.

The horses would be used less and less that year until all the equipment was converted to tractor mode. We had now become completely modernized in our working of the land and milking.

In the fall of 1955, the horses would now begin a well-deserved retirement package and enjoy a life of leisure for their remaining years.

Retirement was not a happy time for them.

You could almost feel their sadness from no longer being part of the work effort. Especially during haying and threshing. They would become restless, and often follow the empty wagon and tractor out into the field and return with the wagonloads of tractor driven hay.

We would still use them for recreational hay rides in the summer and fall, and sleigh rides in the winter.

We would often ride them bare back. During these recreational times both horses and human participants would once again bond and enjoy the activity.

They enjoyed the very important role they had played in our life on the farm and provided a dimension to farming that few will experience today.

I will never forget Frank and Laudie

More Farmland

In 1955, we would add our last 150 acres of farmland to our scope of work which meant we would be actively farming 450 acres in 1956.

Part of it was farmland owned by George Atkins on the south/east corner of Bronte road and the Upper Middle. The rest was part of the Cooper farm and the future site of the Richview golf course.

The Cooper farm was on the west side of Bronte road on the north/west corner of the upper middle.

Now at the ripe old age of 11, I was now considered eligible to add hay cutting, plowing and milking to my duties, which I began in the fall of 1955.

Different Farming Methods 1955

By this time, we would be putting over 8,000 bales of hay and straw in the barn. We would load the wagons by hand and using a three-pronged fork. It was hard work and would build many muscles.

It became a contest to see who could best pitch the bales to the upper levels on the wagon.

One or two would load the bales onto the wagon, one would build the load, while one drove the tractor. The builder would use a bale hook to place the bales on the load.

In the barn, the hay fork system would no longer be used with the introduction of bales. In its place, we would use a chain link conveyor.

The conveyor was slightly larger than the width of a bale with upright hooks on the chain to carry the bale.

The sides were about six-inches high to hold the bale in place when travelling up into the hay or straw mow.

The conveyor was about 20 – 30 feet long and driven by a small non-sparking electric motor.

It would be placed on the top of the wagon and moved and re-positioned many times as the wagon emptied and the number of bales in the hay mow grew.

We mostly loaded the bales into the conveyor by hand using the bale hook, unless it was far enough away need to use a pitch fork.

The bales travelled to their required location in the mow and bale hooks were used to remove them from the conveyor and to build the mow. We still would salt the mow after each load.

New Games Created with Bales

The bales would create a new mode of enjoyment for Brian and me as we would build many secret tunnels and forts in the hay and straw mows. It would mean many hours of fun and laughter.

Our dogs would travel through the tunnels and emerge from the other end in proud triumph.

Cash Crops

With the availability of 450 Acres of land, we began planting cash crops of corn and wheat and barley.

We would rotate these new crops along with the oats and wheat on all the fields.

The Recreational areas

The recreational areas were once again brought back to their days of glory after the storm. The sides of the pond were once again groomed, and grass was re-planted.

The soil swept from the fields left the bottom of the pond very muddy. Getting in and out was not fun as it meant crawling through several inches of it.

We built a dock to avoid the mud when getting in and out. We built rafts to drift out and enjoy the water. We continued our games riding the logs.

Visits from more Relatives

This summer we would see more cousins including Ron and John Shillum. Russell now a budding farmer himself, would return for his annual country experience.

Gail would return this year for a longer visit. Another cousin Peter would also come and stay for a short time.

Winter 1955

Skating would continue to be one of our main winter activities. We would often return to the fields and skate the long natural rink that stretched several fields back.

Christmas 1955

This was one of the other Christmases that would also stand out in my memory. It was the year I would get my single shot 12-gauge shotgun. I would also get a Large Chemistry Set and microscope kit that would open a whole new world for me.

There would be many trips to Allen's Pharmacy in Bronte to obtain many test tubes, flasks, beakers and chemicals.

Mr. Allen, the pharmacist and owner took great interest in my chemistry activities and often would have many used test tubes and other items that he provided free.

One of my projects in 1956 would be making gunpowder for a firework display on the May 24 weekend. The display was a fizzle and burned one of the fence posts so bad it had to be replaced.

MEMORIES OF 1956

The New School

One of the biggest changes for me in 1956, would be starting the last part of grade Six at the new school (Palermo Public #3). My brother Brian had started school in the St. Luke's Parish hall, and he would never attend the one room, but joined me in the new school.

In comparison with the old one room school, to me, it was enormous. There were four classrooms and each class room taught two grades. The new school was L-shaped with three classrooms down the north side and a fourth beside the third on the south/west end.

Grades 1 and 2 were at the far east end with 3 and 4 next travelling west. Then came the principal's office followed by 5 and 6 on the north side. Beside 5&6, and on the south side was 7&8.

Seven and eight and five and six, were separated with a retractable wall which was opened for assemblies.

The first half of grade six was spent in the one room school with the last part in the new school. My remaining public-school days of seven and eight would also be spent here.

My younger brother Brian would see his last year in the church parish hall, and in the spring of 1956, he moved to the new school. He would complete the rest of grade 3 and all of grades 4 to 8 in the new school.

Busing

Since the students came from greater distances buses were introduced at this point. In the morning, we had it easy as we were at the end of the bus route and there would be a short trip to school.

In the evening, the bus took the same route as in the morning which added about an hour to the trip home.

Since the bus would pass by the Back Concession travelling up Bronte Road (Hwy 25), we would usually get off there and walk the rest of the way home.

During the nice weather, we would often ride our bikes to and from school. This gave us the chance to start collecting pop bottles on the way home from school.

We would use the money to buy candy at the Palermo General store.

New School Activities

Once a week grades seven and eight were bussed to a larger school where manual training was available for the boys and home economics was available for the girls.

Elvis Presley

It was during these trips to manual training, I first heard about Elvis Presley. All the girls were talking about him. Later in 1956 I would watch his first appearance on the Ed Sullivan show on September 9 and become a lifelong fan.

Ed Sullivan was one of the shows on TV that we could stay past our regular bedtime of 9:00 O'clock. Yes, at age 12, I had a curfew.

Baseball would still be the main pastime during recess and lunch.

We would begin our interschool baseball competition travelling to each of the schools in our district. My position was usually left or centre field.

The Farm Work in 1956

Preparation for Seeding

In the spring, as soon as the fields were ready, I was now 12 and would do my share of the plowing, discing and harrowing in preparation for seeding. This would take place after school and on weekends.

Planting

My job included getting the seed and fertilizer out to the appropriate field and loading it into the seed drill. My dad and Bob would still do the seeding.

Haying

I would begin my involvement in the afternoons and evenings during the school week and it would continue all weekend.

Once school was out, I would take part in all hay cutting, raking and baling. All of us along with whoever was visiting at the time, would look after bringing the hay into the barn.

Harvesting the Grain

When the combining started we would all look after getting the grain into the grainery. Most of the baling of the straw was still done by my older brother Bob and my dad. We all would take part in bringing in the bales of straw.

Preparing the Land

In the fall of 1956, I would once again become involved in the plowing. I would help with the discing and preparation of the land for seeding as I had previously done.

My Paper Route

The late spring of 1956 would see the beginning of my career as a paperboy delivering *"The Toronto Telegram"*. It would be something that I could do on my way home from school.

In the beginning, it would not take up much time as there were only a few customers. In the summer, I would still have time to do my normal farm chores while building my clientele.

Starting with a customer base of about six, I continued to add customers. By the end of summer had reached around 57 daily Toronto Telegram customers plus additional local weekend customers.

The Farm Boy becomes The Paper Boy

The route started in the south end of the village of Palermo and went both east and west on Hwy 5 (Dundas).

It went about ½ to ¾ of a mile in each direction. It then travelled north up Hwy 25 (Bronte Rd.) to the top of the hill past our road the Back Concession.

Coming back down to the Back concession, I would first go east to the end of the road (dead end at 16-mile creek). I would now travel west, past our house to the town line.

On weekends I would travel north on the town line for week-end customers.

It would take 2 1/2 hours after school each night and a lot of riding. Once home (around 5:30), I would start my farm chores.

The paper route was fine until winter arrived. With the snow, I would now depend on my dad to drive me to all my customers. Shortly into the second winter month, it became too much (for my dad) and I ended my first job outside of the farm.

Future Benefits

It was here I had an early taste of selling, and I liked it. Later in life I would become a salesman and would sell for others as well as my own companies.

At that point, unlike my paper route, I would do the driving in the snow.

The Pond

This summer would see the invasion of turtles and muskrats. We did not worry about them until we found our first snapping turtle. It was napping on the bank. It was about 18 inches plus in diameter with large spikes on its tail.

To catch it, we dangled a large stick in front of it. The turtle grabbed the stick in its mouth and would not let go.

We moved it away from the pond and dropped it into a burlap bag used for grain and took it away.

Even after catching the snapping turtle and transporting him several miles away, the desire to go swimming had diminished with the discovery.

Summer Visits

The visits from our cousins would continue again this year. Both Russell and Gail would return for their annual visits.

MEMORIES OF 1957

Management Changes

We would now experience a new management structure. In 1957, we were still operating around 400 acres of farmland and were now milking around 35 cows.

My older brother Bob was now 19 and had begun co-managing the various operations of the farm along with my dad. It appeared that Bob would eventually be running the farm.

The mornings and weekends still saw my dad involved in the milking along with Bob.

While Brian and I were attending school, during the week, we had only a few morning duties, such as putting down the straw for the bedding of the cows and bringing in eggs and milk.

In the evening, Brian and I would often alternate getting the cows from the pasture and herd them into the coral ready to start milking.

We would put fresh straw down again for the bedding and collect the eggs. In the fall and winter, we would also put down hay morning and night for food when the pastures were done for the year.

My brother Bob would start the evening milking and very often I would help finish before my dad came home. I would often spell him off during evening milking to allow him to go on a date.

Farm Duties

Everything continued much as it had during the previous years with us all taking our part in the sharing of farm duties.

Pond Skating

Ice presented no problem with snapping turtles, and it would continue for many years to come.

The Pond when Full
Looking North up the lane at our bush

Brian and I are once again playing hockey on the now huge pond surface. No shovelling necessary here, but it would take a mild day to get rid of the ripples in the ice.

Back to the Slopes on the Farm

Our New Recreation

For Christmas 1957 we would look out on our front lawn to see a blue luxury fiberglass boat parked under the tree in the snow. This would change our entertainment life on the farm forever.

MEMORIES OF 1958

The Farm

In February of 1958, my brother Bob would get married and he and his wife Deanna would live at the farmhouse while we were building their new house.

My older Brother Bob and his new wife Deanna

My dad had severed off the south west corner of the farm and financed the building of the house as a wedding present.

There would be few other projects beyond the house this year as we all would help in its construction. All our duties on the farm would continue pretty much as they had been the two years before.

Hired Help

During this summer of 58, we would also hire my best friend Bruce Ebbs from just down the road. It would be great fun to work together.

None of us would ever forget my father's call to action after a break.

*It was: **"To your Stations Men"**.*

This call would get its worse reception on very hot days, when you just knew the hay or straw would go down your neck and stick to your skin. Removing one's shirt only seemed to make things worse.

And who could forget the rise and shine song my dad would sing.

"Oh, how I hate to get up in the morning, oh how I love to stay in bed. It's time to start your day, it's time to get the hay.

You got to get up, you got to get up, you got to get up in the morning."

The middle lyrics would change to suit the occasion, but the message was the same.

Luckily my friend Bruce would not be subjected to the rise and shine call or he probably would have quit and gone home.

That would be a call for his sons and any of our cousins who were visiting.

Recreation 1958

We would make many trips to Bronte to launch our new boat into Lake Ontario that year.

That year with the new management, my brother Bob would run the farm for two weeks while the rest of us took a holiday. Gullwing Lake that year would be the beginning of many visits that would take place in the years to follow.

Packed and Ready to Go Summer 1958

Below Our Vacation Spot Gull Wing Lake

Public School - My Grade 8 Graduation

In June of 1958 I would see the end of public school, and with it the end of my school days in Palermo. I also saw the end of our community togetherness.

Above: My best Friend Bruce Ebbs is 2nd and I am 3
From the left side front row
Below: Signatures and ages of my graduating classmates

Next Year High School

We would soon travel many miles to attend our high school "Thomas A Blakelock" in Oakville. I did not realize at the time what the changes lay ahead and what the new high school would bring.

We would soon lose the close friendships that we enjoyed in our one room and small village school, with all our friends in the same room.

We would soon be separated into seven different Grade Nines (9A to 9G) and separate home rooms. The sense of community was never the same as everyone developed new friends and interests.

The one-room public school still holds my fondest school memories, with those early years all in the one-room being by far the best.

My life would soon change as I entered High School and the next chapter in my life would begin.

OTHER FARM MEMORIES

It was not all Work

Every year there would be many activities on the farm that happened during the fifties. The activities listed here were not allocated to any one year, so I have created a separate chapter for them.

SPRING ACTIVITIES

Spring meant one thing as the snow melted and rivers started flowing again. Fishing season would soon arrive.

Spring also would bring Easter and coloured eggs, egg hunts and chocolate from the Easter Bunny all celebrated to Gene Autry's *"Here Comes Peter Cotton Tail*

The annual Shillum Easter egg hunt would always have to wait until we got home from church.

With spring, the valleys in the fields turned into small streams, where we had great fun sailing makeshift boats. Rainfalls would create large rivers that needed respect, and we would sail larger boats.

We would get our rubber boots full of water many times.

Fishing at 12 Mile and 16 Mile Creeks

Our Back Concession was an eventual dead end in both directions. To the west was the twelve-mile creek and to the east was the sixteen-mile creek.

My fishing adventure would begin the night before with the watering of our lawn. Close to midnight, I would begin my hunt for worms using my flashlight. I always collected a large supply.

12-Mile Creek

Travelling west on the Back Concession, I would cross the town line and travel about half to three quarters of a mile into Nelson Township to where the road became a pathway.

At one time, there had been a bridge over the creek and there was an old trail down to the river's edge. Once there, I would decide which direction would be that day's adventure.

Both directions offered a wilderness to discover. The red clay cliffs would rise perhaps as high as 100 feet and then disappear into a gradual slope and flat land with many types of bushes, flowers and weeds.

Every turn would offer a new adventure. Travelling west for several miles would eventually end up at the remains of an old mill. It had not been used for many years and was in a bad state. I remember finding an old milling wheel with a square hole in the centre. It was too heavy to lift, let alone move.

There were a few other parts of foundations that meant some sort of attempt to build a community many years before. It was now overgrown with trees.

My second option was travelling east from the old road and along the river. It would end at a large wooden railway bridge.

The Railway Bridge

The railway bridge over the creek was usually the eastern most part of my explorations. This was probably because there was a perfect fishing and camping spot just before it.

I would spend many mornings and afternoons there fishing with bobbers and my worms. I would usually bring a lunch prepared by my mom and my thermos of vinegar and honey.

This area became my own special domain. I cleared a portion of the riverbank close to the river and gathered stones to create a fireplace.

I was very careful as the Toronto memories of the burning garage and Captain Sheldon were vivid reminders of my early carelessness and lack of respect for fire.

On occasions, I would cook one of the perch, bass or trout that I caught. If I was lucky there would be enough to take home for everyone. One rule prevailed. If you catch them, you must clean them.

Crossing the Bridge

Sometimes I would go directly to my spot, but it meant crossing the railway bridge. I would put my ear on the track to listen for oncoming trains.

It was a long way to the other side (about 350 - 450 feet) with no railings on either side. There were only a couple small platforms about three feet by three feet that hung over the edge of the bridge.

From their appearance, I did not ever want to test how strong or safe they really were.

As I was crossing, I could see the river below between the open railway ties. Moving too quickly would cause dizziness as the open space on the sides and below rushed by.

Only once in all the times I crossed, did I encounter a train. Luckily, I was 2/3 of the way across. I had to walk a lot quicker than normal and finally run to cover the final part of the crossing.

I jumped over the side and down about six feet, just avoiding the contact of the train. The conductor was sounding the train's loud whistle all the way across the bridge as the train approached me and passed by.

After that my Crossings were few

I would spend most of my time exploring the 12-mile creek but never went past the bridge as it continued south. The creek would eventually end up in Bronte and Lake Ontario.

16-Mile Creek

Travelling East on the Back Concession and crossing over Hwy 25, it was a much shorter distance to the 16-mile Creek. This creek eventually flowed into Oakville.

The landscape was different as the road ended with a path down the banks to a more open area than the 12-mile creek. For me it also did not provide as much adventure as the 12-mile creek and my visits would be less frequent.

The fishing never seemed as productive as the 12-mile and produced fewer bass or perch. The trout were fun to catch but seemed more elusive.

As the 16-mile creek flowed under Dundas (Hwy 5), it would be like the 12-mile with high banks. The area there was much wider at river level and had been the site of an early settlement. There were the ruins of many buildings to explore.

SUMMER ACTIVITIES

Camping

We would enjoy camping and had three locations where we would pitch our tents. In our younger years, we would pitch our tent right next to the house, beside the front and back sheds.

Mom and Dad would be within voice range and mid-night snacks, breakfast and the washroom would be just steps away.

Soon we would camp by the pond in the summer and bring our snacks and often our breakfast supplies in a cooler. Here we would enjoy all the pond sounds and have a campfire.

When we got used to being away from the house and got a little more daring, we would pitch our tent in the bush, at the back of our property.

There was a spot part way into the bush that was perfect to pitch tents. Here we felt totally isolated surrounded by bush and the new sounds would often see us rushing back to the safety of the house.

Most often the bush camping occurred when our cousins were visiting and there was safety in numbers (usually 5 or 6 people). On a few occasions, we would hold part of a family reunion at the bush with campfires games of baseball and football.

At evenings end, the adults would return to the comfort of the house and the younger crowd would remain for the adventure in the wilderness.

We joined cubs and scouts and there would be many weekends where the group would set up their tents and enjoy the bush. There would often be seven or eight tents.

We would use the small field in front of the bush. One year we held a scout jamboree with about 30 - 40 tents in the same field. My dad was very busy that year transporting everyone plus supplies back and forth by wagon with a little hay on it, treating everyone to a farm hayride as well.

Once cubs and scouts ended in Palermo, my dad found himself driving us to Bronte once a week to Sea Scouts.

Our Dogs

Laddie and Lassie came with the farm and would become great companions for everyone.

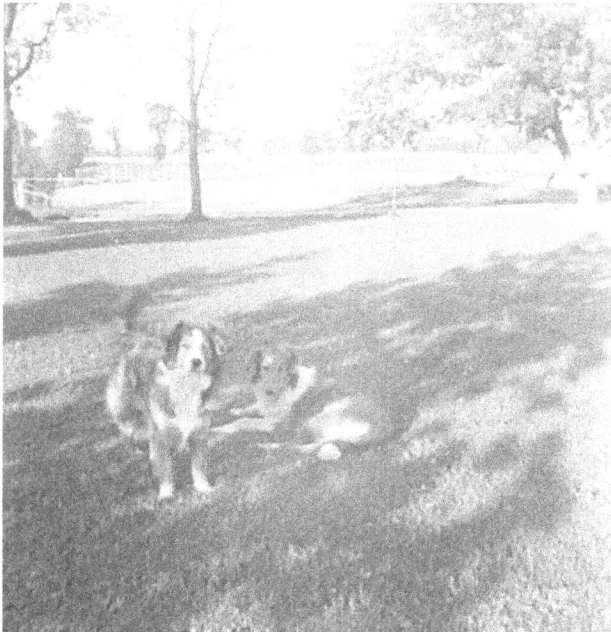

Laddie and Lassie on the Front Lawn

Unfortunately, we would only have Lassie for three years as she was killed by an unfeeling hunters' bullet. We searched the farm for many weeks with no luck. Several months later we would find her in our bush and carried the remains back to bury her behind the house.

Mac McGill Laddie and my Dad on the West Lawn

Laddie in the Clover

Laddie in the Snow

Family Reunions Mom's side and Dad's side

The farm became the annual host for family reunions on both sides. We were the only ones in the family who had moved to the country and everyone wanted the farm experience.

The reunions would usually last the whole weekend. Often uncles and cousins wanted to take part in some activity relating to farm work. To provide a short experience involving whatever crop was being harvested, would see a short excursion to satisfy their thirst.

Most times there would be a hay-ride back to the bush and a campfire where we roasted hotdogs and toasted marshmallows. On the way people would hop off the wagon to grab cherries, apples, pears or plumbs from the trees in the lane.

Back at the house there were many games, swimming in the pond and games of hide and seek and homefree or buzz-off, that we played with the cousins.

When we had corn in the front fields, it made a great area for these games and the building of mazes and supplied our corn roasts.

221

The Trips to Toronto with my Mom

One area that became an ongoing outing for us, were the trips to Toronto with our mom to shop as Simpsons and Eatons. While at Eatons we would always visit our Toronto baby sitter Mrs. Taylor who worked in the cafeteria.

After down town, we would take the subway and travel north to the Eglington stop. We would often walk to the park at the bottom of Roselawn and pause for a packed lunch.

The park ran the entire width between Eglington and Roselawn. It was where we used to play when we lived in Toronto.

After that, we would visit some stores on the westward walk up Eglington to do the grocery shopping where my mom had shopped during the time we had lived just blocks away.

Occasionally we made another stop before Grocery shopping. It was one that we would never look forward to. On the corner of Avenue Rd. and Eglington was the dentist's office. My dad had a dental plan at work, and we would have many visits there over the years.

When our visit to the park or dentist's office was done, we would do the grocery shopping. When it was done, we would all sit in the front window of the grocery store and wait for my dad to pick us up after his work.

The bi-monthly trips would continue for many years and we would take the day off school, which was always exciting.

FALL ACTIVITIES

Fall was a Special time of year with the leaves turning and the colours that were everywhere in the country.

The distinctive odour of the fallen leaves gave notice that winter would soon be coming. We would rake the leaves into large piles and run and jump into them. We would also build forts.

Later we would have fires of burning leaves. The aroma of the burning leaves is something special in my childhood memories on the farm.

Fall was time for fall plowing and harvesting our pumpkins for Halloween. We would travel to all our neighbours in the country for our traditional treats.

We then would head to Palermo where we could walk from house to house. After driving from farm to farm earlier, Palermo was a gold mine.

Halloween would see a gathering at the community hall for dancing and prizes for the best costume.

WINTER ACTICVITIES

There was nothing like the first snowfall that would turn everything white. I remember often stepping out into the moonlight and listening to the silence of the falling snow.

The reflection of the moon on the snow was a magical moment that seemed to be inviting Santa to pay a visit.

Christmas Visits to Toronto

The trips to Toronto were especially exciting at Christmas time. Both Eatons and Simpsons would go overboard with decorations, rides and of course, Pumpkinhead and Santa Clause. There was the annual Eatons Santa Clause parade that we never missed.

Christmas Trees from Toronto

For three or four years from 1950 to around 1953, we would purchase our tree from a former neighbour on Roselawn Ave.

It was usually on the day we went to a Family Christmas concert put on by the (UCT) United Commercial Travelers. My dad was a member.

Christmases on the Farm

Christmas was always filled with visits to and from Santa. Somehow Santa knew we would be at each place we visited, and always had presents for us.

We had our trips to Eatons and Simpsons in Toronto, the UCT party, the Palermo School concert, the Church party in the Parish Hall and the party at the Atkins.

And then the best of all, was the visit by Santa to our own house on Christmas eve. We had it made.

My mom would decorate the kitchen, living room and dining room with strings of garland from the corners of each room and connecting the four strands in the centre. Here, she would hang bells, tinsel and red bows.

In later years, I would gather branches of pine trees from the Britton's bush because it was much closer than our own bush. I would use the branches to decorate all the windows.

We would hang tinsel and ornaments on the branches.

Our tree and Table Decorations

In Those Later Years

We would start adding flood lights around the house, lights in the windows and put lights on all the evergreen trees by the house.

The baking was a highlight every year. My mom made two white and two dark Christmas cakes for the family. There were also homemade mincemeat squares, tarts, apple pies, and her melt in your mouth shortbread.

We would upgrade from our chickens to a turkey from one of our neighbours'. We had squash, potatoes, carrots, corn and more from our garden. I will never forget and my mom's famous dressing.

There were always plenty of candies, chocolates and even home-made ice cream. We would even make our own fudge on the old wood stove in the kitchen as it seemed more like an old fashion Christmas.

The dinners during threshing were close but never would reach the level of Christmas day on the farm.

All these treats, except the meat and perishables were stored in in the enclosed cool front porch. When someone disappeared, they were usually sneaking some goodies.

Mom and Dad Helping Families in Need

Both my mom and dad were generous people. Christmas was one of the times when they would pull out the stops. There were families in Toronto and in Palermo that were less fortunate than we were.

Every year, my parents would supply these families with some of my mom's home-made Christmas cake, mincemeat, shortbread, cookies, eggs, frozen chickens, a few dozen eggs and beef from our freezer along with toys for their children.

They would wrap everything, so the children did not know what was happening and deliver everything in large bags. It was a gesture they kept very private, and it showed the true meaning of Christmas.

They would also help these families throughout the year, but Christmas was always special.

Christmas Parties in Stratford

Every year for many years we would travel to Stratford on Christmas day evening, after the milking was done. We would attend the annual family Christmas get together on my mom's side.

While in town we would also visit my dad's mom and his sisters who still lived there. For many years the get-togethers would be held in my grandparents' house.

It was a large 3 story red brick house across the road from the old Stratford Railway Station. My grandmother used to run restaurant in the train station and bake for it.

There would always be lots of her great baking and treats. That is one place where my mom obtained her culinary skills.

The Great Christmas Milking Expedition

One of the annual traditions would be the men getting up at three in the morning to go back to the farm, to do the morning milking. After the milking was done they would all return and carry on with the party.

Everyone wanted to take part, and for a few years, there was no room for me. My uncles and older cousins would fill every available spot in the two-car expedition.

I always felt that I was missing out
on a great adventure.

Our family would usually leave when it was time to do the evening milking. Most times we would keep the cows waiting a bit.

The Milton Fall Fair

On a farm, the fall fair meant extra activities as we usually would show one or more of our calves. We were members of the local 4H club.

It was a 3 to 4-day event and often meant camping on the fair grounds to look after our entry or entries. We had converted the old highway truck to allow transportation of animals.

Truck waiting to load the animals

We would bring our food, tents, and of course hay, straw and grain for the livestock. Everything was packed into the back of the truck.

On the back Lawn

My dad demonstrating how to show the calf

A closer view of the calf

We got in free and would roam the livestock area, watch the competitions and visit all the exhibits. We would also try our luck at the many chances to win stuffed animals, but usually left with a cheap plastic whistle or other useless item. It was all fun.

Our winning entry in the Fall Fair

My new Enterprise

About 1957, I decided to raise hound dogs. Perhaps influenced by the Elvis Presley song Hound dog man.

My enterprise soon turned into a nightmare with over 15 pups to feed and no sales. The puppies were turning into dogs and my savings from my farm chores were shrinking quickly.

Then a strange thing happened. One day I went out to feed the now young dogs, and all but four or five of the 15 were gone. The next day they all were gone. I feared they had been stolen.

Soon after, neighbours for miles around began calling saying one or two dogs had been literally left on their doorstep.

They had seen my large hound dog pups for sale sign out front with phone number.

It seems the two mothers had decided enough was enough and distributed their litters around the countryside for free. My hound dog enterprise days were over. My dad had the females fixed and once again their future on the farm was secure.

One of my hounds

Delivering Calves

Many times, over the years I would be called upon (mostly in the middle of the night) to help deliver calves. The request usually meant it was a difficult birth.

Often, we would need to tie a rope around a leg or legs, sometimes a head and pull. It could sometimes take just minutes with the additional help or might be an hour or even two.

We would usually emerge from the barn triumphantly tired. The experience is something I will never forget.

Not all Deliveries Ended Successfully

Only once after many hours of effort, did we need to call Doc Heslop the local veterinarian in Palermo to assist.

On this occasion, after many additional unsuccessful hours, we had to destroy the cow as the delivery was impossible.

Later we would Discover Why.

It was a calf with two heads, eight legs and one body. It was very rare and found a place "I think" at the University of Guelph.

More Farm Pictures

Our first year doing our own Threshing

On the left side is the threshing machine connected to our tractor. It is blowing the straw into the barn.

In the middle is my older brother Bob taking a picture of Brian and Laddie standing in the clover. Behind them you can see our hay-loader and wagon.

I am taking the picture of all the above.

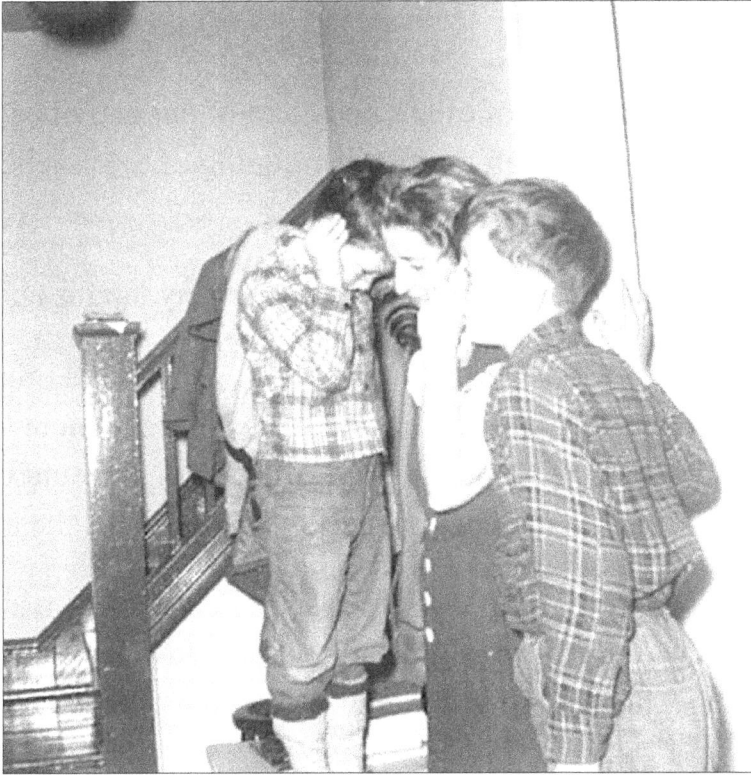

Our new rotary Dial Phone
Brian, Mom, and me

No more hand cranking

We are standing in the front hallway. Behind us you can see the stairway to the second floor.

Must have been an important call as we are all trying to listen to the conversation.

My Practical Jokes

After reading an early proof of my book and of our activities on the farm, Brian asked why I left out the mentioning of the practical jokes that I used to play on him.

He began to refresh my memory and we had many laughs about them as I made my notes for this addition to the book.

Being the older brother and having a weird sense of humour, I would play many practical jokes on him. Part of our chores would be putting down the hay from the upper portion of the barn to feed the animals.

The second level of the barn was always spooky with the wind howling through the cracks of the barn boards. It was usually dusk or early morning when we were required to do these chores.

This offered a great atmosphere to orchestrate my pranks. I used to fill pants and shirts full of hay and tie them together. Often, I added a Halloween mask for further effect.

I would place the figure at strategic locations at floor level and found an excuse to send Brian to that location.

I would often position a flashlight to shine on it highlighting the mask. It worked every time as I would soon hear a scream of terror and Brian would come running.

Sometimes I would climb up into the hay mow where I had stashed the figure. After throwing down the first lot of hay, I would throw the figure over the edge of the mow, yelling as it fell to the floor.

Brian would usually call my name in panic and run to figure on the floor. It worked a couple of times, but soon there was more anger than concern.

Sometimes as Brian watched TV, I would appear in my scary Halloween mask in the window shining the flash light on the mask. I would then bang on the window and watch him flee in terror.

After reminiscing these past events, and having a few more laughs, I admitted that I had a weird sense of humor back then and added the above to my book.

Another prank we both played on our dad was to switch his Rye and ginger ale when he left to take care of something. It was usually about a third full and we placed a similar glass of cider vinegar with an ice cube in its place.

Upon returning, it was usually bottoms up followed by some spitting and swearing. After a few successful times he wisely checked his drink by sniffing it first.

One time our dad participated in this prank when one of our uncles was visiting. We all had a laugh. The word spread and anyone visiting would soon check first before taking a gulp from an unattended glass.

What did I Gain from Life on the Farm

It was not only the memories and the chance to experience life on the farm in the 1950's, it was the experience and responsibilities that we were all taught to handle.

We learned the responsibilities of looking after animals in our care. It was feeding them and making sure they had proper bedding. It was looking after their needs, if they were sick or injured.

We learned respect for equipment both maintenance and repair but also the most important issues of safety. There was always an element of danger and possible loss of life or severe injury when operating farm equipment.

This respect would follow all of us throughout our entire lives right to this day.

We became innovative with the need to repair equipment in the field to keep working. We always had an almost magical toolbox with all sorts of bits and pieces of steel, nuts and bolts and always our valuable fence pliers.

We would often travel to the fence lines to find a bit of wood or cut some wire from the fence to make a repair. We became very self-reliant to use what was available. To this day I have always had fence pliers in my tool box.

We learned respect for nature and wildlife and the need to look after the environment. I believe our mom and dad chose well in providing the opportunity to learn and grow through life on the farm.

I believe my parents chose the perfect farm for us to experience life on a farm. They also could not have picked a better community than their selection of Palermo, Ontario

The Shillum Homestead 1950 to Mid-1970's

A Recent Picture

The above is very much how the farm looked during our 25 years stay here. So far, it has remained untouched by the advancing developments that are now only one concession south.

PALERMO REVISITED IN 2017

While memories do not change, they often fade with time. When they are revisited; the new reality of change, can often be a shock to the system and the heart.

Such was the case when I would re-visit Palermo during the writing of this book. After almost 50 years of not living there and16 years of not visiting, I would find that the picturesque small village was no more.

In its place were apartment buildings and suburbia.

In all naivety, I had returned to refresh my memories for the writing of this book. It was supposed to be the return to my roots and verification my childhood memories.

Instead I would come face to face with the reality that the small rural community, was gone forever. In its place I would find the disregard and destruction of history and heritage.

It would be obvious that progress (greed and indifference) had won. I am saddened by the fact that too often the people doing the developing win, while our history is destroyed.

I have pieced together a glimpse of old Palermo from the 1950's. Most of the information was found on line through a few sites and those generously provided by the

Trafalgar Palermo and Oakville Heritage Societies.

There were also many telephone conversations

Thank You Both for your help.

LAYOUT OF COMMUNITY AS I KNEW IT 1950's

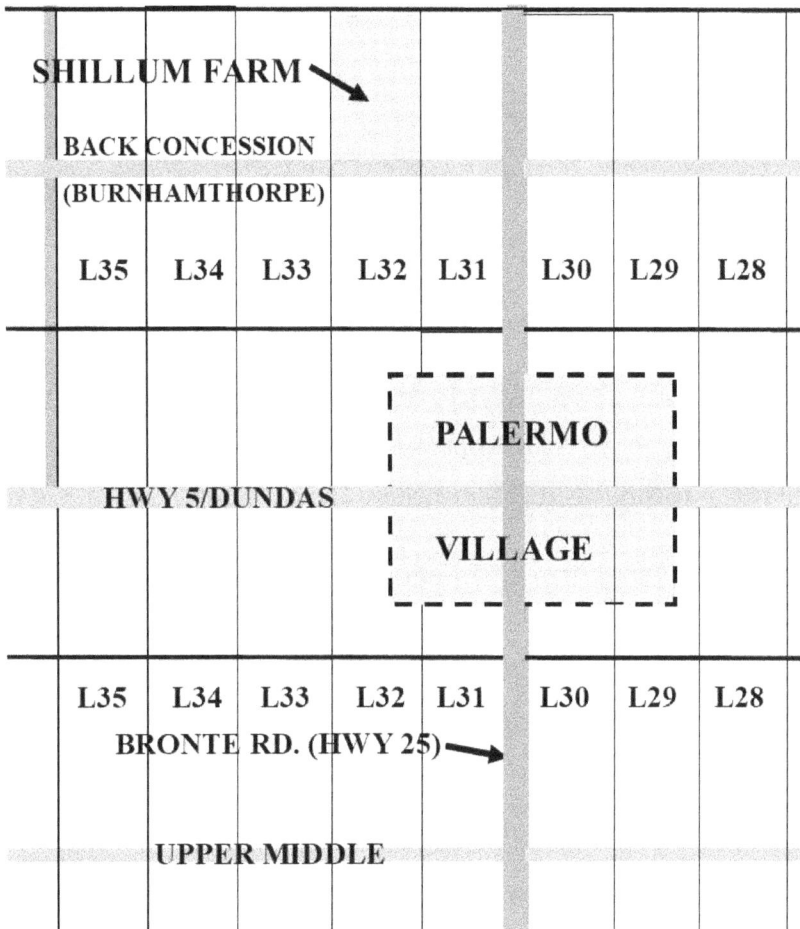

SHILLUM FARM ↘							
BACK CONCESSION							
(BURNHAMTHORPE)							
L35	L34	L33	L32	L31	L30	L29	L28
			PALERMO				
HWY 5/DUNDAS			VILLAGE				
L35	L34	L33	L32	L31	L30	L29	L28
BRONTE RD. (HWY 25) →							
UPPER MIDDLE							

LIST OF RESIDENTS IN 1950s

North side Back Concession (Burnhamthorpe)

Lot 35 Scotland / Lot 34 Proud / Lot 33 Wendover /

Lot 32 Shillum / Lot 31 H – Higgnet /, Part Lot31 Hendrickson, Fuller & Britton / Lot 30 Wettlaufer /

South side of Back Concession (Burnhamthorpe)

Lot 35 VanSickle / Lots 34 & 35 not known / Lot 32 Bullock / Lot 31 Britton / Lot 30 & 29Pope / 28 & 27 not known by me.

North Side of Dundas (Hwy 5)

Lot 35 VanSickle / Lots 34 & L33 Lazy Pat / Lots 32 & 31 Britton / Lots 31 & 30, Part 29 - VILLAGE

South of Dundas (Hwy 5) & Others

Lot 34 R. Smith, / St Lukes Church Lots 31 & 30, Part Lot 29 - VILLAGE

Adding Palermo

My original intent was to provide information about Palermo in the 1950's for this book. Unfortunately, many buildings and homes are no longer there today in 2018.

While searching for pictures, I discovered some very interesting bits of historical information about Palermo and area. The following is not meant to be a complete history of the area; but merely, some background of Palermo's early beginnings.

The Beginning of Palermo

The settling of the area began around 1805 with many of the original settlers being United Empire Loyalists.

The name United Empire Loyalists was given to those who remained loyal to the British crown during the American War of Independence.

The Loyalists were original settlers of the 13 American colonies and many joined the British army and if not killed in battle, suffered confiscation of property, persecution and imprisonment.

Trafalgar was an area settled by many Loyalists who were given land by the British Crown. Usually the land was in 200 Acre parcels or more depending on one's service.

David Hagar (a United Empire Loyalist) was granted property in 1804 by the crown and left it to his son Lawrence.

During my research showed that the original name for Palermo was *Hagar Town* named after Lawrence Hagar who was one of the first settlers in 1805.

The name of *Hagar Town* remained until 1837 when the first post office was opened. At that time a public meeting was held to choose a new name.

Doctor William Cobban proposed the name *Palermo t*o honour Admiral Lord Horatio Nelson, Duke of Palermo and it was adopted.

Dundas Street was one of the oldest and most significant east-west overland routes between Toronto and western Canada. The village was also at the intersection of the road travelling north from Bronte to Milton (Bronte Rd).

In 1881 a telephone line starting in Toronto would pass through Palermo, Waterdown and Springfield on its way to Hamilton. H.W. Switzer became the first Bell agent. In 1900, L. Hagar became the agent for Bell.

In 1909, the Palermo telephone Association was started and would service 50 subscribers in the area before being purchased by Bell in 1911. W.S. Wood was then placed in charge of Bells Public telephone in Palermo.

The first foundry was built by Jacob Lawrence in 1842. As shown on the next page it consisted of the Woodshop, Pattern house, Store House and paint Shop.

In 1847 it was awarded third best Canadian Plow at the Provincial Agricultural fair in Hamilton.

TOWN OF PALERMO in 1878

Palermo Agricultural Works 1878

Source: Halton County Atlas

SHORT HISTORY OF PALERMO

Palermo was once a thriving settlement. The Lawrence Foundry and Agricultural Works was established here in 1842. By the 1870's, Palermo was an important supplier of charcoal to factories and blacksmiths in Hamilton.

It also had a wagon shop, blacksmith shop, harness shop, hotel, brick schoolhouse, several churches, telegraph company office and large drill-shed.

It was also known for the abundant wildlife in the area, including wolves, bears and deer. The findings of a study noted that Palermo Village is the oldest remaining settlement (1806) in the present-day town of Oakville.

This was because settlement along the Dundas Street military road from Toronto to Dundas was opened some 20 years prior to the settlements at the ports of Oakville and Bronte.

Dundas Street was a major east west transportation route in the 19th century and Palermo prospered both as a stop for travellers, and as the centre of the surrounding agricultural area.

The passing of Highway 25 through the centre of the village, which linked Bronte and Milton, made Palermo an important junction for overland travellers in the 19th century.

Many of the buildings in the village were constructed during this period of prosperity.

Information Source:

Palermo Village, Oakville: A Heritage Resources Review and Strategy

Location, Location

Unfortunately for the village, the main reason that accounted for its success, would eventually become a major factor leading to its demise.

In the 1950's, the increasing traffic on Dundas and Bronte Rd. created the need to widen both roads caused the beginning of the end for the historic village. The by-pass around the village core would come too late to save many of these homes and buildings.

Coupled with that, the failure to obtain Heritage status for the village allowed the removal and demolishing of many historical buildings.

The Changes that I Saw

One of the early buildings affected by these changes that I would witness, would be the white frame home on the south/east corner of Dundas and Bronte Rd. In 1955, it would be relocated to make way for a Fina gas station.

Soon after I would see the general store on the north east corner of Dundas and Bronte Rd. demolished to make way for road improvements.

I would also witness the destructive fire in 1955, that would destroy the foundry on the east side of Bronte Rd. south of Dundas.

Some Others Lost

- The community hall on the west side of Bronte Rd. and south of Dundas would also be demolished for road widening.

- The first building registered in the village in 1822 at 2488 Bronte Rd, would fall into disrepair and eventually collapsed in 2007.

- St. Lukes Church would escape demolition by being moved and added a huge section to the original church. Not sure what happened to the old Parish Hall or rectory.

- The white frame house moved from the south west corner of Dundas and Bronte Rd. in 1955, would eventually be demolished in the name of progress.

- The Georgian 2-storey on south side of 1495 Bronte Rd. 1960's

- The Gothic Revival South side of Dundas west of 25 in the 1990's

- The Implement store West of Bronte Rd. South side of Dundas was demolished in the 1960's

- Georgian Cottage south side of Dundas and west of Bronte Rd. was relocated in 1950's.

How I Remember the Village of Palermo

MY 1950's MAP VILLAGE of PALERMO

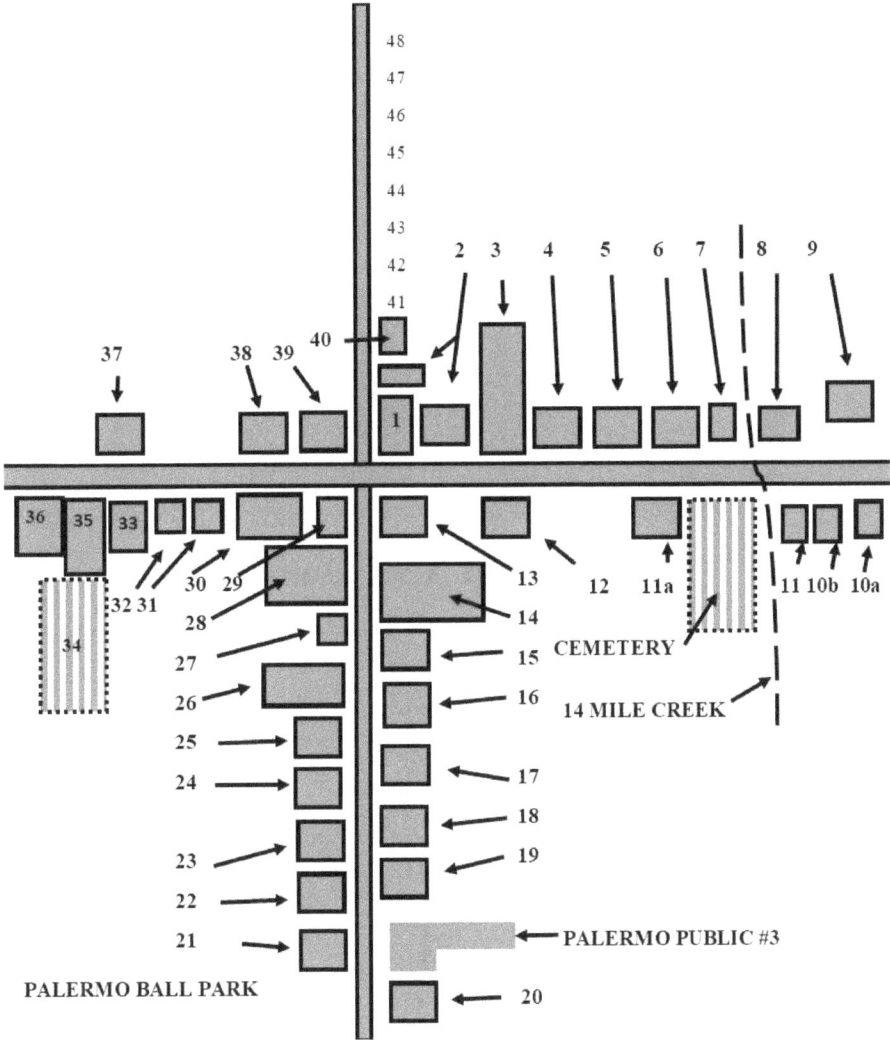

48
47
46
45
44
43
42
41

2   3   4   5   6   7   8   9

37   38   39   40

1

36   35   33   30   29
            32 31   28
34   27
            26
            25
            24
            23
            22
            21

13
14
15
16
17
18
19

12   11a   11 10b 10a

CEMETERY

14 MILE CREEK

PALERMO PUBLIC #3

PALERMO BALL PARK

20

THE 1950'S BUILDINGS OF PALERMO

AREA ONE of VILLAGE

Corner Hwy 5 and Hwy 25
Looking East late 1940's early 1950's

My Map Area One

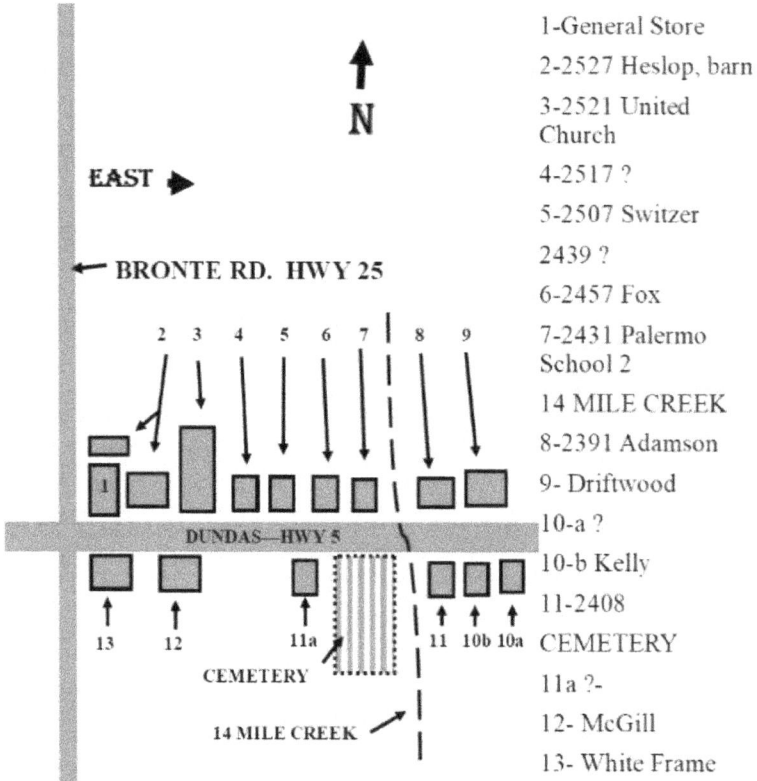

1-General Store

2-2527 Heslop, barn

3-2521 United Church

4-2517 ?

5-2507 Switzer

2439 ?

6-2457 Fox

7-2431 Palermo School 2

14 MILE CREEK

8-2391 Adamson

9- Driftwood

10-a ?

10-b Kelly

11-2408

CEMETERY

11a ?-

12- McGill

13- White Frame

Palermo General Store early 50's

This is where we got our work gloves, and other farming needs. We would pick up our mail as there was no delivery to the farm. My dad also sold his eggs here.

My brother Brian and I would collect pop bottles and cash them in for 2 cents each and buy treats. That was when penny candy was really a penny. We would get licorice cigars and pipes for 1 cent each. Pop was 10 cents a bottle (including deposit).

A Short History

First store built and owned by Lawrence Hagar in 1830. It was known as Hagar's old red store. The store in the picture was built by Clubine and Johnson in 1843. It was sold to Harvey Switzer in 1846

Other owners include James Dobson, G.S. Wood, and R.B McGill. It was demolished when Bronte Rd was widened in the 50's. A new store would be opened on the west side of Bronte Rd. just south of Dundas.

2527 Dundas (Doc Heslop)
It was located on the east side of the Store.

The house shown above was Doc Heslop's home as I knew it. He was the local veterinarian and would make many trips to our farm.

A Short History

The home was build around 1870 by Jonathan Hagar, the son of Lawrence Hagar. It was considered as the third Hagar house. At age 25 Jonathan Hagar would leave Palermo to mine gold in California and Australia. He returned in 1857 when his father died and would eventually build this home.

Tennis at back of the House around 1900

Note: United church to the left

2521 Dundas Palermo United Church

Next to Doc Heslop and shown above was and still is the United Church. Although we would not attend here for worship, we did join their *"Young Peoples Group"*.

A Short History

Built in 1867 in what was known then as Hagar Town. The church was dedicated by Bishop Richardson after being given the keys by Dr. Anson Buck who was a leading figure in raising money for its construction.

2517 Dundas next home – no picture or information

2507 Dundas - Built 1868
Switzer House

Not sure who lived here in the 1950's

A Short History

Harvey Morris Switzer moved to Palermo in 1844. He was the Postmaster in Palermo, owned the corner store at one time, was a county magistrate, and a commissioner in the court of the Queen's Bench.

In 1861 he purchased 24 Acres of Lot 30, Conc. 1 NDS and completed the building of the above house in 1868.

2457 Dundas – Built in 1825

This farm was next to the Switzer House travelling east and was the home of the grandparents of my school mates Ken and Ed Fox.

A Short History

Original owner of the property was John Shaw. Purchased by the Fox family around 1900 who lived there till the mid 1970's.

2431 Dundas - Built1942

Palermo Public #2

Shown above is the one-room school where I would attend grades one to five and half of 6 before moving to the new school at 2451 Bronte Rd in the village.

A Short History

Records show the land (3/4 Acre) was acquired from John Shaw by William Henry Hagar and sold to the School trusties for $30 around 1876.

The school shown above was the second school known to have been built on this property in 1942. The one before it was built in 1875 and was struck by lightning during a storm and destroyed by fire.

Although the first school in Palermo was built around 1844, its location could have been across the road from this one.

2391 Dundas
Built between 1842 and 1845

The Adamson's lived on the other side of the small 14-mile creek on the east side of the school in the 1950's. This was originally another Hagar home.

No Picture of "The Driftwood"

2408 Dundas - Built 1925

The above house was on the south side of Dundas.

The United Church Cemetery

Established 1812

This was on the South side of Dundas across from Palermo Public #2. Here looking north, you can see the schoolhouse in the distance. The original owner Charles Teetzel sold the property for use as a cemetery forever. In 1812 a log house was built on the property. In 1818 the first internment took place.

The McGill House

It was on the south side of Dundas opposite the United church. It was the home of the McGill's who owned the General Store after the Woods. It was either moved or demolished.

Corner House

Included are two pictures taken in 1955 when the white house on the corner was moved, providing a different view of Palermo in 1955.

View from South side of Dundas looking West

On the left is part of the foundry roof behind the shed. On the right side behind the house is a faint view of the farm Implement Dealer.

View from Dundas Looking East

Above, is a view of the white house from the north edge of Dundas on the other side (west side) of Bronte Rd. To the left you can see the General Store.

I have read in my research that the white frame was once one of two stores east of Bronte Road on opposite corners of Dundas that were operating in the early 1900's.

In the top left corner of the picture, you can see part of the White Rose sign for Britton's Garage and gas station. It was on the north/west corner of Dundas and Bronte Rd. at the time this picture was taken.

Before the White Rose was the Thompson Hotel built around 1860.

Early 1900's
Corner- Hwy 5 and Hwy 25 - Looking South

My Map Area Two

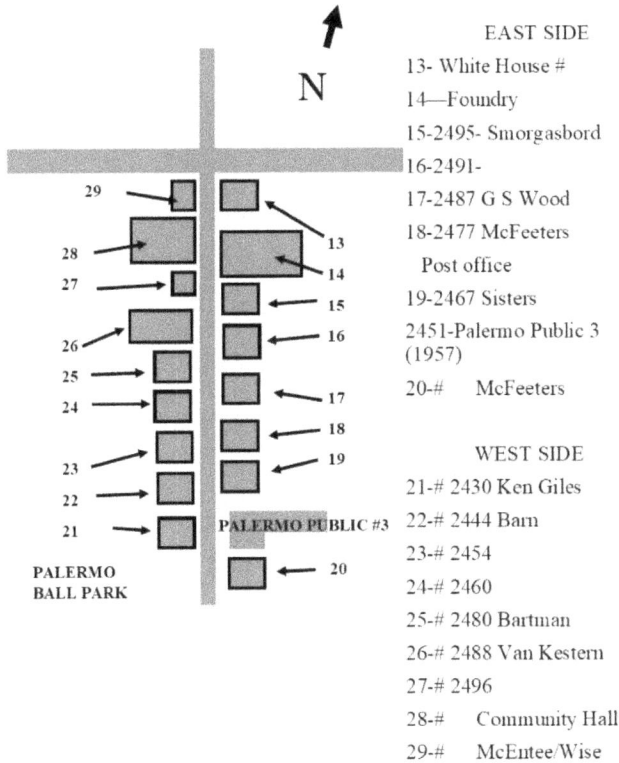

N

EAST SIDE

13- White House #

14—Foundry

15-2495- Smorgasbord

16-2491-

17-2487 G S Wood

18-2477 McFeeters
  Post office

19-2467 Sisters

2451-Palermo Public 3 (1957)

20-#   McFeeters

WEST SIDE

21-# 2430 Ken Giles

22-# 2444 Barn

23-# 2454

24-# 2460

25-# 2480 Bartman

26-# 2488 Van Kestern

27-# 2496

28-#   Community Hall

29-#   McEntee/Wise

PALERMO PUBLIC #3

PALERMO BALL PARK

257

Corner White Frame being moved 1955

**The Remaining part of the Foundry
Built in 1842 – Destroyed by Fire 1955**

The history of this property was provided earlier in the section on Palermo.

2495 Bronte Rd. – Built 1825

The house at 2495 was the original home of Dr. Anson Buck who was one of the original settlers of Palermo. In the 1950's it was a restaurant we called the Smorgasbord.

Brian worked here for a while as a server. I would never become a patron and missed a true dining experience of 1950's Palermo. It is still a dining spot and it is my intention to filially become a customer.

A Short History

The house was built by Dr. Buck who was a descendant of a United Empire Loyalist. It was built in 1825 and his home and launching point for his many house calls made by horse and buggy.

2491 Bronte Rd. – Date Built unknown

2487 Bronte Rd - Built in 1920

G.S. Wood and wife Ethel raised their family here. They also owned the Palermo General Store and Post Office after James Dobson and would later sell it to R.B. (Mac) McGill.

Pictured on the next page is Mrs. G.S. Wood talking with a customer in the Palermo general store and post office where she was a part time assistant.

Ethel Wood in the Palermo General Store.

2477 Bronte Rd – Built 1870

The building at 2477 Bronte Rd became the post office when the old general store was demolished. For a short while they also carried some groceries and candy.

When the general store at Bronte Rd. and Dundas closed, the telephone switchboard moved to this location. The bell switchboard would be operated from here by Ethel Wood who lived next door.

2467 Bronte Rd – Built 1913

All I know about this house was that two sisters lived here.in the 1950's. They were a must on Halloween because of the treats.

Palermo Public # 3 Built 1955

I attended the 4-room school until 1958 when I graduated grade eight.

The school was used as a public school until late 1960' and eventually sold in the early 1970's and demolished to make way for a new Portuguese Catholic church and school.

Bronte Rd looking South at Dundas

House below is the same as the one on far right above

House South West Corner

Located on the south/west corner of Bronte Rd. and Dundas, I knew it as the home of the McEntee's in 1950's. It would eventually be moved west on Dundas (same side) with the widening of the highway. **Note:** the restaurant in the background on left side. (Dr. Buck's)

A Short History

Records show that about 1816 this property was owned and farmed by Benjamin Smith. He also built his carriage works at 2488 Bronte Rd.

Community Hall – Built 1912

Above is the old community centre located just south of the corner house. It would eventually be torn down when Bronte Rd. was widened in 1973.

A Short History

This property was donated to the community early 1900's by Henry Heeks for the building of the community centre. John Dearing and Lawrence Hagar also shown as grantors of the first part. The building of the hall was funded by the people of Palermo.

2496 Bronte Rd. – Built 1945

2488 Bronte Rd.

A Short History

The land for the above house was granted to Benjamin Smith (a carriage maker) in 1806. The house was built in 1822 and was the first house on record in the village of Palermo. It fell into disrepair and collapsed in 2007.

2488 Bronte Rd in Better Days

2480 Bronte Rd. - Built 1890
Above: Bartman House
Below: Bartman Blacksmith Shop

2460 Bronte Rd. – Built 1875

2440 Ken Giles House

Ken Giles did our combining after we no longer harvested our grain with a binder and threshing machine. He also drove the school bus.

Corner Hwy 5 and Hwy 25
Looking South/West late 1950's

My Map Area Three

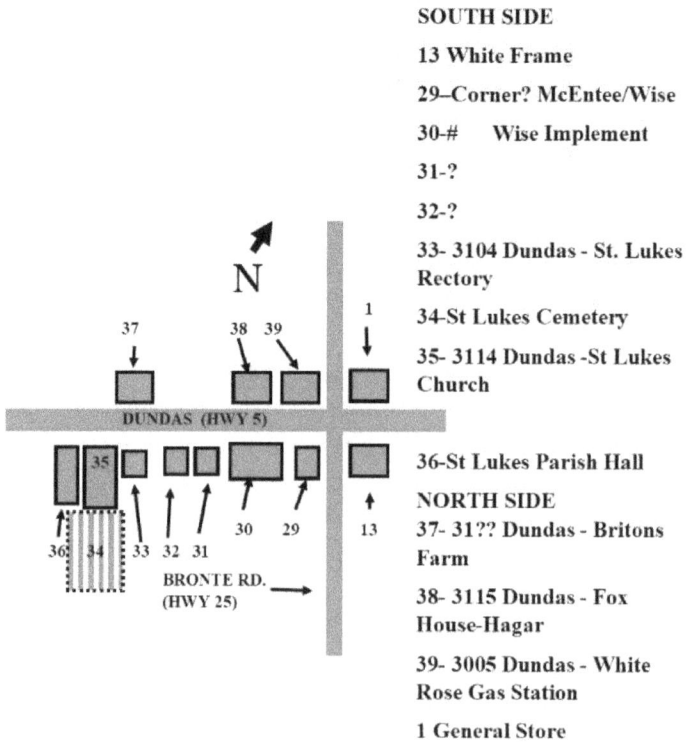

SOUTH SIDE

13 White Frame

29–Corner? McEntee/Wise

30-#   Wise Implement

31-?

32-?

33- 3104 Dundas - St. Lukes Rectory

34-St Lukes Cemetery

35- 3114 Dundas -St Lukes Church

36-St Lukes Parish Hall

NORTH SIDE

37- 31?? Dundas - Britons Farm

38- 3115 Dundas - Fox House-Hagar

39- 3005 Dundas - White Rose Gas Station

1 General Store

House on South West Corner

Palermo Farm Implement Supply early 50's

This business was located on the south side of Dundas next to the brick house on the corner shown above it. I remember sitting in the car with my brother Brian while my dad was inside negotiating his latest farm implement purchase.

St. Lukes

Further west on the south side was the church rectory, St Lukes Church and the Parish hall and Cemetery. We would attend church here as well as many other social activities in the 1950's at the Parish Hall (shown partially here to the right).

3114 Dundas Front View of Church in 1950's

Back View of St. Lukes Church in 1950's

A Short History

Construction began in 1845 under the guidance of William Peacock. William Peacock was the first Justice of the Peace in Halton County and started giving prayer sessions in his home.

The first worship took place March 1, 1846 and the church was officially consecrated on June 22, 1868 after the debt of construction was paid.

The rectory was built in 1908 by reverend R.C. Weaver. The belfry was erected in 1932 with the bell supplied by the Lawrence foundry

There were several more homes after the Parish Hall but could not find any information on them.

Reg Smith Welder

The property of Reg Smith Lot 34 was further west on the South side of Dundas in Trafalgar Township.

Lot 34 South of Dundas

Over the years we would make many trips to the welding shop of Reg Smith shown above. He would make repairs on our equipment and build items we had designed for our own use.

A Short History

The Smith family were United Empire Loyalists and obtained the 200 Acre parcel in 1831.

White Rose Gas Station 1955

This is the only picture that I was able to find of Britton's White Rose Gas Station. It is on the right side. There are several vehicles on the lot but unfortunately the quality of the picture was poor.

The Thompson Hotel around 1900
Built around 1860
Before the White Rose

Before the White rose gas station was the Thompson Hotel built in 1860. In the foreground of the picture is the general store which is on the north/east corner of Dundas Street and Bronte Road.

Behind the store is the Hotel on the north west corner. Just past the hotel is the horse stables and a partial view of the Hagar home which is shown below.

3015 Dundas – Built 1848

The Fox house above as I knew it, was Originally a Hagar home mentioned and partially seen in the distance on the previous page.

Next to the White Rose on the north side of Dundas and shown above was 3015 Dundas. In the 1950's I knew it as the home of Ed and Ken Fox.

Their Grandparents owned the farm on the west side of Palermo Public School on Dundas.

3069 Dundas St. (Britton's early 50's)

The house above was part of the farm owned by the Britons in the 1950's. They would eventually sell the farm and close the gas station.

Corner Hwy 5 and Hwy 25 - Looking North

Corner view in the early 1900's remained very much the same in 1950 except for the mode of transportation. (Horse and buggy) The roads would be paved, and the trees were larger.

My Map Area Four

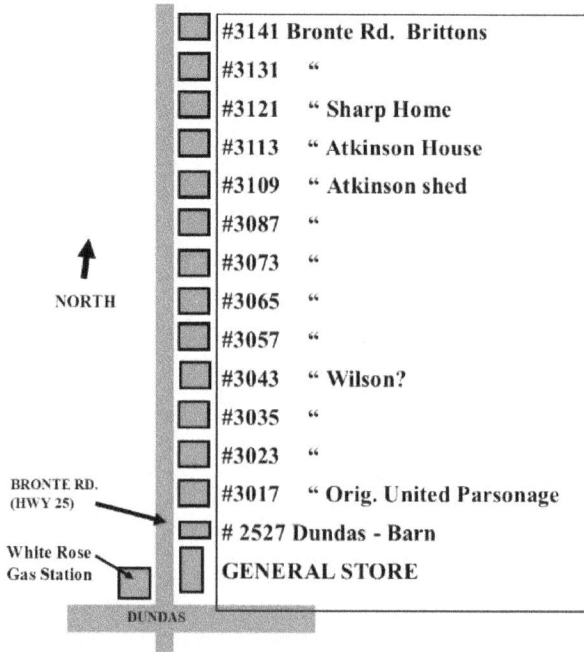

NORTH

#3141 Bronte Rd. Brittons
#3131 "
#3121 " Sharp Home
#3113 " Atkinson House
#3109 " Atkinson shed
#3087 "
#3073 "
#3065 "
#3057 "
#3043 " Wilson?
#3035 "
#3023 "
#3017 " Orig. United Parsonage
2527 Dundas - Barn
GENERAL STORE

BRONTE RD. (HWY 25)

White Rose Gas Station

DUNDAS

There were no homes in the village of Palermo on Bronte Rd. north of the White Rose station. Further north close to the back concession, would be a home owned by the Britton's.

In gathering information for the east side of Bronte Rd. travelling north from Dundas, I was not able to find many pictures of homes.

Instead I listed property addresses shown on a November 2008 Review and Strategy document prepared by the Heritage Planning Division of the town of Oakville.

The following provides pictures and information of only three homes.

Address 2527 Dundas

The picture above is taken in 1955 from a position just north of Dundas and facing south behind the old general store and Doc Heslop's house to the left. It was known as the Hagar barn.

3017 Bronte Rd. Built 1880

This was the old United Church Rectory originally built beside the Methodist (United) church in 1880. At the time it was decorated and furnished by the Ladies Aids of the Palermo circuit. In 1912 it was sold by the church and moved to 3017 Bronte Rd.

The Wilson House

Harry and Wilma Wilson lived here in the 1950's. House was built by Wilma's father Ernest Henderson. In 1952 Harry was hired as a Trafalgar Township policeman by Fred Oliver.

3113 Bronte Rd.

Built between 1910 and 1930

I considered this house at 3113 to be at the northern most part of the village. This would be located about the halfway point on the way north to the back concession where we lived.

Summary

The community life as I had known it during my first 8 years in Palermo from 1950 to 1958 is represented by the contents of this book.

Many changes have occurred since 1958 and my early years on the farm and Palermo experience in the 1950's.

Palermo has now lost its individual unique identity and has become part of Oakville.

I hope this book will help preserve some memories of Palermo Ontario and rural life experienced by a farmboy in the 1950's.

Thanks to all who helped me with the resources to
Present those very Special early years

AS A FARMBOY
IN 1950'S PALERMO, ONTARIO

The research for pictures and information produced much more than I originally intended for this book. I decided to include the information as I felt it gave more depth to the village.

What I provided was only a portion of the fascinating story of the area. The information provided has only scratched the surface and has captured my interest to find out more.

Perhaps it will become the subject of a future book.

Wayne Shillum - Author

www.ingramcontent.com/pod-product-compliance
Lightning Source LLC
Chambersburg PA
CBHW081323090426

42737CB00017B/3018